CAN CHOCOLATE COME OUT TO PLAY?

To Mattia -
Thanks for the inspiration
of L'uomo Nero!! Enjoy!

Jay Bellamy

Jay

Copyright © 2020 by Jay Bellamy

All right reserved. No part of this book may be used or reproduced by any means, graphic, electronic, or mechanical, including photocopying, recording, taping or by any information storage retrieval system without the written permission of the author except in the case of brief quotations embodies in critical article and reviews.

Because of the dynamic nature of the Internet, any web addresses or links contained in this book may have changed since publication and may no longer be valid. The reviews expressed in this work are solely those of the author and do not necessarily reflect the views of the publisher, and the publisher hereby disclaims any responsibility for them.

Dedications

To a much loved mother, the late Iris Bellamy who entered into eternal sleep August 2016. We walked a difficult journey together Mum, and now your journey is at an end as will mine be one day. You are fondly remembered and greatly missed by many.

Also

To the memory of Horace White who died in September 2014 outside the Whittington Hospital in Highgate.

Horace was an eccentric and well known personality around North Finchley in London. He is fondly remembered for knowing and recalling the names of all who came into contact with him and for his trademark greeting: "The best of luck!" delivered in a booming but jovial voice.

He was often to be seen sitting on the pavement outside either Sainsbury's supermarket or McDonald's drawing pictures with crayons.

Thanks to an online petition, which attracted over 6,000 signatures, not only has the council placed a bench outside Sainsbury's in his memory, but they have since built a memorial play area and gardens in the grounds of the Grange Estate where Horace lived.

And to the Lost Rainbow Children:

To the casual listener or observer, whenever we hear of another child taken from loving and distraught parents, by a cruel and uncaring criminal, we care not whether the child is black, brown or white.

As one, we recoil in horror, shock and revulsion when we think of the innocence of the taken, the awful fact that their future has been so abruptly curtailed, and of the never-ending pain and deep sense of loss endured by those left behind to grieve.

Even though we will never meet the individuals to offer them kind words of comfort personally, our hearts are inevitably touched because through us all there runs a rainbow thread of humanity which knows only compassion.

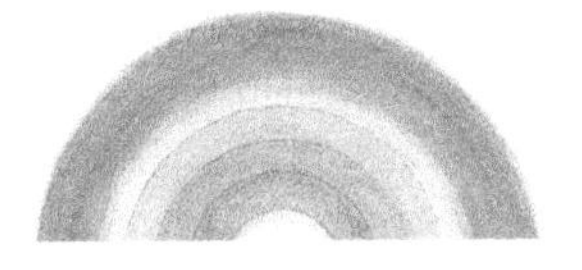

To the memory of:

Jasmine Beckford, Nicola Fellows, Karen Haddaway, Stephen Lawrence, Holly Wells, Jessica Chapman, Damilola Taylor, Ben Needham, Victoria Climbié, Baby P, Madeline McCann and all of the other lost souls no longer with us.

CHAPTER ONE

The Island I Left Behind

Petrified Tree and boat on Barbados Beach.
By Jay Bellamy

It is believed that it was the Portuguese who first came to Barbados in or around 1527. It was at this time that the island was named Los Barbados or 'Bearded Ones' by the sea captain Pedro A. Campos. It was so named, presumably, after the island's fig trees which have a bearded appearance.

History further suggests that Barbados was later discovered by mistake in May 1625 by a merchant, Captain John Powell after his vessel 'The Olive Blossom' was blown off course and ended up in a small inlet of shallow water at the edge of the island. Upon going ashore, the uninhabited land was immediately claimed for the British and was initially named St James Town and later Jamestown after King James the First of England. In February 1627, this became the site of the first settlement in Barbados and the town was eventually renamed Hole town after the shallow body of water or 'hole' where ships could land safely.

The heritage that subsequently evolved was hugely influenced by the geography and geology of the Island. Barbados is just as much an Atlantic Island as she is a West Indian

Island. Barbados is a coral island. Unlike the neighbouring islands of St Vincent, St Lucia and Dominica which have populations related to indigenous Amerindian people, Barbados has no such group. The Island had been bereft of its native population in the early sixteenth century having fallen victim to Spanish slave-raiding expeditions from larger northern Islands.

An often-overlooked factor when assessing the routes of Barbadian heritage is the composition of the island's population during the first 4 decades following settlement in 1627. Today, with an overwhelmingly large black population in excess of 90% we tend to forget that nearly 400 years ago these figures were reversed and that over 90% of the island's population was of European extraction being made up of English, Scots, Welsh and Irish, as well as Spanish and Portuguese, Sephardic Jews together with a smattering of French and Dutch. It is believed that the Barbadian accent started to emerge during this period influenced by West Country and Irish speakers.

The seasonal forest that covered the island prior to English colonisation in 1647 was cut down to accommodate the shift to sugar and vegetable cultivation. Barbados essentially became one large cultivated garden with over 500 plantations each with its own windmill and almost 200 farms where crops such as yams, sweet potatoes and pumpkins, could be grown. Other farms took advantage of the rich soil and produced ginger, aloes, maize and even cotton.

CHAPTER TWO

The Red Legs of Barbados

From the earliest part of the 17th century, the Caribbean was regarded as a source of immense wealth, power and opportunity. The English, in particular, saw this as the ideal environment in which to grow crops, tobacco and cotton, but for this, they needed field workers and servants.

In the winter of 1636, a ship bearing 60 men and women left Kinsale in County Cork in Ireland and headed for the Caribbean. Those on board were destined to become indentured servants on the plantations of Barbados and would be the eventual forebears of an often forgotten race who still live on the island today. The Redlegs.

In all, more than 50'000 'white slaves', including a supplement of Scots were transported from Ireland to Barbados, many of them poor folk or prisoners captured by Oliver Cromwell during the conflicts in Ireland and Scotland. These white slaves became known as Redlegs due to the blistering effect the sun had on their fair skin.

Even today, the descendants of the original Redlegs are often referred to as poor whites or Baccras and it remains somewhat incongruous that there could actually exist a white race in Barbados that could even be considered to be poor in a country where the word 'white' has always been synonymous with success and power for centuries.

Redlegs are now a diminishing but a close-knit poor white community that can be found predominantly in the New Castle district of St John parish but also in parts of St Vincent and Grenada and it is possible that they may be some way related to the Black Irish communities in Monserrat.

By 1680 most of these people were free having served their purpose as indentured servants and it is believed that while many stayed and became farmers or artisans, many others emigrated to neighbouring islands.

CHAPTER THREE

The Legacy of Bussa

During the second half of the 17th Century, thousands of West Africans were brought onto the island on a yearly basis to work as enslaved labourers. They came from a variety of ethnicities, speaking different languages from varying cultural backgrounds. They were regarded solely as the property of their masters, the landowners and planters of the day. Their cultural heritage was forcibly repressed, regarded purely as "merchandise" to be bought, sold and used by their owners as they wished. No human or civil rights were afforded nor any financial reward for the work they did. There were, however, some cases where favoured female slaves were taken to live in the households of particular plantation owners. Many of these women were even granted eventual freedom along with the children borne out of the liaisons, creating a new class of "Free Coloureds."

The statue of Bussa the slave, erected at Emancipation roundabout, is a reminder of the slave revolt in April 1816. Bussa's Rebellion as it is known, was the first of three large-scale uprisings which shook public faith in the slave trade and which eventually led to emancipation and the abolition of slavery in Barbados in 1834.

The bronze statue which symbolises the "breaking of chains", was crafted in 1985 by Bajan sculptor Karl Broodhagen.

The rebellion began on the night of Easter Sunday, April 1816 with cane fields being burned in the parish of St Philip and expanded swiftly to neighbouring districts to such an extent that landowners were forced to flee to Bridgetown, the colonial capital in order to preserve life and limb.

Despite the rage of battle which ensued over two days, the uprising was eventually quelled with the 400 or so slaves being suppressed and finally overpowered by the local militia comprised of the West India Regiment, a division of the British army, together with British Imperial troops, ironically made up of many slave soldiers.

Bussa himself was killed by the militia and despite the scope of the rebellion, it was reported that only two whites died in the fray.

Following the outcome of an investigation by the administration five months later, the Governor of Barbados, Sir James Leigh, reported that approximately 250 people had been either executed or sentenced to death, while another 170 were deported to other British Colonies in the Caribbean.

Bussa, widely regarded as having been the architect of the uprising of 1816, is among those whose lives are now celebrated on National Heroes' Day on April the 28th of each year. Also among the number of notable contributors to the history of Barbados is Sarah Ann Gill, remembered as a staunch anti-slavery protestor and supporter of Methodism, along with Samuel Jackman Prescod who became the first person of African descent to be elected to the Parliament of Barbados in 1843.

Both Gill and Jackman were children of mixed parentage having had black mothers and white fathers. It is worth mentioning that although both of them "bore little or no marks of Negro complexion" as quoted, they were, even as Free Coloureds, subjected to many examples of discrimination endemic at that time in Barbados.

Statue of Bussa the slave
located at the junction of ABC
Highway and Highway 5.

Illustration by jay Bellamy.

The Creole form of English spoken on the Island had evolved enough by the middle of the 18th century to attract the attention of visitors to the island. George Washington in 1751 observed that high born ladies "by ill custom try to affect the negro style", and Edward Thompson in 1756 remarked that white Barbadian women were often heard swearing in a "most vulgar and corrupted dialect."

Barbados was very well defended by a chain of 42 coastal forts and the Island became the headquarters of the British in the Eastern Caribbean. Some of the wealth generated by sugar exports was spent on erecting Anglican Churches, one for every Parish with beautiful interior decorations and magnificent stained glass windows.

By the middle of the 17th Century, the Sephardic Jewish community built their own synagogue. Given the name, Nidhe Israel, it remains arguably the oldest in the hemisphere.

Barbados, whilst a very small Island, it is one with an extremely dense population. Over time the character of the Barbadian has adapted and evolved sufficiently to accommodate the specific circumstances of the island. Its harmony and balance are indeed attributes and testimony to its survival and progress.

Today, having gained its independence in November 1966, it is a paradise island flanked on one side by the Caribbean Sea, and on the other by the wild Atlantic Ocean. The natural vegetation is lush and green and the wide variety of vividly beautiful flowers such as bougainvillea, hibiscus and Iolanthe seem to sprout in explosions of colour. Tamarind trees in bloom are everywhere to be seen and visitors to the island are often treated to the sight of troupes of Barbados green monkeys either making their way unhurriedly across a path or leaping through mango trees picking the ripened fruit.

Barbados is also known as The Rum Island and this alcoholic beverage is believed to be the oldest of its kind to be distilled in the Eastern Caribbean. The first commercial variation of this drink is believed to have been produced in Barbados in 1637 which coincided with the rise of the sugar cane industry, which then became the backbone of the Bajan economy well into the 20th Century.

Mount Gay Distilleries, founded in 1703, still produces the oldest brand of rum in the world. Visitors to any of the many such distilleries to be found on the island are advised to be extremely temperate when sampling the beverage in case they suffer what is amusingly known on the island as a "rum fit".

Nowadays, the island economy is far less dependent upon sugar and rum production due to its emergence as a premier tourist destination.

CHAPTER FOUR

Mum

Mum sold her property in London in the autumn of 2012 and repatriated herself back to Barbados.

It should have been a fabulous retirement for her, enjoying the house which she had built 25 years ago in St James. Not so. She now suffers from vascular dementia and it is so awful to see the slow mental decline of a previously boisterous, feisty and even belligerent human being.

After watching my father deteriorate and finally succumb to his own condition, It now became clear that I was losing the battle to hold on to Mum as well. It became difficult to even have a proper conversation with her due to her delusional episodes. She believed that I was there with her most days, even though I lived in London. She often told visitors to her house that I was in the back room, often with two or three women. Sometimes dad was there as well apparently. Neighbours of mum frequently phoned us in London at unholy hours to report that she had been knocking on their door complaining that dad and I were "there again" taking things from the back bedroom.

We had become accustomed to receiving calls from Barbados at all hours enquiring if we are on the Island following reports from Mum that we have "just left the house having stolen a lot of her things."

If not us, then it's that damn Rastafarian man who has a mysterious way of bypassing her locked doors and steals her bread. Apparently he only cuts off a slice on each incursion into the premises. She was constantly changing the locks on the front and back doors. Mind you, she had been doing even that before she left London. We had put it down to increasingly bizarre obsessive behaviour and failing memory.

It was difficult to see her level of confusion so pronounced that it became evident that she was never quite certain which country she was in.

Whenever she returned from visiting Barbados, she would often fly into a rage accusing me of having picked the locks of her bedrooms and taken "stuff", even though the rooms remained locked and she had safely stashed the keys in her luggage and taken them abroad with her.

Strangely, she never could say precisely what was missing.

And then there was the time she accused me of throwing away the urn bearing the ashes of her beloved cat Minnie. She was so convinced that I was guilty of this atrocious act of malevolence that she even threatened to call the police. We tried unsuccessfully to convince her that she must have packed it away in one the barrels of personal items she had shipped overseas.

It came as no surprise to me some months later whilst visiting her in Barbados to come across the treasured urn safely stashed away in a drawer. At this stage, her cognitive abilities were so severely impaired that she would often ask me: "Tell me something – am I in England or in Barbados?". At that point I took the decision to actively instruct airline companies in Barbados NOT to sell her any tickets to travel to London should she turn up at their booking office.

We also managed to take her driving licence and car keys away after she got into the habit of driving down to various banks in Barbados thinking she was going to her UK bank which caused quite a lot of consternation to the staff when she would angrily insist on speaking to staff she knew in London.

If I could level any criticism of Mum, it would be that she was wasn't guarded enough about her accumulated wealth. Having worked extremely hard often in racially charged environments which presented her with many professional challenges to overcome, she revelled in boasting about the amount of money she had acquired and saved, along with the many properties bought and sold during her working life. She took great pleasure in telling friends of the impressive bank balances built up over many years. This somewhat foolhardy honesty or braggadocio attracted many fairweather friends and fawning acolytes who would on occasion seek to borrow sums of money from her which, to her credit, she stubbornly ignored. It is also fair to say that Mum used her financial clout to either reward loyalty from these minions or conversely, punish them by, for example promising to leave them gifted amounts in her Will or removing their names from the document if they erred in any way.

I wasn't exempt from these actions either as my name was added and removed many times over the years depending on whether she approved or disapproved of my own perceived loyalty or disloyalty.

As hardworking and dedicated to her profession as she was, it would be fair to say that Mum was no angel. She swore like a trooper, as they say, and was never slow to use the "F" or "C" words. Many people felt the scourge of her tongue in a hail of venomous expletives if they challenged or displeased her in any way and one would be wrong to believe that I was exempt from her verbal onslaughts. As her cognitive abilities diminished, her bursts of rage would become more intense and frequent.

CHAPTER FIVE

Stranger in a strange land

I arrived in England on a cold, damp and foggy morning in 1958. My parents met me and my guardian, who had travelled with me from Barbados, at Euston station. I was just 8 years old and I remember shivering in this strange environment as the icy winds bit through my inappropriate clothing. My eyes watered as I blinked, and my ears were assailed by the clatter of huge, noisy train carriages as they sped by and crowds of people hurried back and forth in all directions. No kites fluttering lazily high up against an azure background or the sound of cockerels trumpeting the arrival of a new day. The blue skies and warm sunshine of the Caribbean suddenly felt very far away.

I remember my mother sweeping me up in her arms and smothering me, all the while covering my face in kisses and weeping. Dad was less demonstrative but I have to assume that he was equally pleased to see that I had arrived safely.

They had arrived in England a year earlier, having left me in the care of Mum's family while they paved the way for a new life in this apparent jewel of the Commonwealth. They settled in rented accommodation in Ipswich, Suffolk. The place we lived in was called The Warren in Lacey Street, and the ever-changing group of tenants were a polyglot of West Indians, Poles and Ukrainians. Mum found work sewing in a clothing factory whilst Dad found employment in engineering companies manufacturing tools. He wasn't suited to this type of industrial work having been a teacher and agricultural instructor from the age of 20. I learned much later that he found it much harder to find work than Mum did. Dad was a highly intelligent, proud, but somewhat insecure man who had always struggled with his own personal demons.

He recounted how on their arrival. They were walking through the airport lounge and were greeted by derisive calls **of "Monkey, Monkey!"**, from a group of white travellers in the arrivals hall. I don't think he ever recovered from that offensive welcome. He simply didn't have the mental toughness to endure such a fierce and totally unexpected onslaught. We didn't know at the time, but Dad was already suffering from the early stages of paranoid schizophrenia, having been discharged early from the army. Even then he was struggling with the pressures of daily life, such as forming and maintaining relationships at work and holding down jobs, while Mum, on the other hand exuded confidence and determination. She never had a problem finding work, sometimes holding down two or three part-time jobs as a seamstress or working in bottling factories. Just as well because dad was frequently laid off following disagreements with the foremen at the engineering firms he was employed at. He always felt people were picking on him.

As the years went by, Mum would eventually carve out a niche for herself in the nursing profession, rising through the ranks from auxiliary level and up to a matron, nurse manager, and head of training.

I would describe my relationship with mum as one where I loved and respected her greatly, especially for her sheer determination to escape from an abusive relationship and then work tirelessly to become an achiever. On a personal level, I would describe her as a mother who felt so much devotion to her only son that she never really let go of the little boy in him. Being an only child often brings its own pressures and in mum's case, I know that she would have loved to have had another child and I too would have liked a sibling as I have to admit that I suffered a degree of loneliness as a result. I suspect that she was desperate for me to willingly attach myself to her apron strings, something which I resisted fiercely, preferring to be my own man and make my own decisions. I recall one day her telling me: ***"never trust any woman, because none of them are any damn good!"*** As a result of that, I am sure that she never truly accepted any of my choice of partners and saw them all as rivals for her affection in some way, which of course, they were not. As a consequence in the latter stages of her life, particularly as the effects of vascular dementia took hold, I know that she often saw me as an enemy, the fact of which has left me with much sadness, but that is how this debilitating illness tears families apart.

CHAPTER SIX

Thomas

Around the age of 9, I remember befriending a young white lad who was of similar age to myself. His name was Thomas and he often knocked at the house for me to go out and play. Most of our time was spent roaming the woods at the rear of The Warren, chasing rabbits or firing catapults at them, although we never actually hit one. It was a valued friendship and I can honestly say that I didn't even register that there was a difference between us though our skins were different colours. Sadly, that friendship came to an abrupt end when my parents decided two years later to move down to London. In later years, through my teens and even as an adult, I often wondered what became of Thomas. And yes, I have to admit, there was often a sense of loss at losing contact with someone who had become an important part of my early life.

It wasn't until many years later, in my fifties to be exact that during a conversation with my ageing mother whilst having a meal at a restaurant that I remarked: **"I wonder what became of Thomas - You remember Thomas, don't you Mum"?**

It's strange how a person with cognitive impairment may not recall a conversation they had a couple of hours ago, but are able to remember an incident from even sixty years previous in detail. This is symptomatic of the acute deterioration of the brain cells responsible for short term memory.

Her reply surprised me. She replied: **"Oh yes. Do you know – he used to knock on the front door for you and ask: *Can Chocolate come out to play Mrs. Bellamy?"***

Mum laughed heartily as she recalled my little friend's visits and promptly continued eating her meal.

I have to admit that for quite a few seconds I was speechless. I just could not understand why the little friend I had lost and of whom

I often had such fond memories, could have uttered such thoughtless and cruel words and for quite some time, perhaps days, the hurt festered like an angry sore and perhaps I even hated him for a brief moment. Was my friend a racist? At that age?

I struggled with these thoughts for quite a while until, at last, I began to think more rationally. Those words weren't Thomas's. I understood. He was merely repeating the words spoken by his parents or at least someone in his household. I could almost hear an adult saying: **"Why don't you go and see if your little Chocolate friend wants to play, Thomas!"**

It was hard at first to even comprehend that while two youngsters played and rode their scooters together and chased rabbits through the woods, cardboard holsters and gunbelt around our waists like cowboys, firing our cap guns at them, that there could be parents with views of such a racially biased nature.

Observation and experience has taught me that young children of all colours and backgrounds will interact happily with each other, oblivious of their differences, until an adult either points out the differences or sows a seed of doubt in an impressionable young mind.

To this day, even under severe provocation or in the face of extremely vitriolic, racist abuse, while I have defended myself both verbally AND physically, I can't recall ever having brought a person's colour or race into my response. That doesn't make me a paragon of virtue because there may have been times when I've considered saying something more extreme. My view is and has always been that an ignorant, bigoted individual is no less or more so due to their race, colour or religion and that includes those of my own race. Why would I lower myself to the same gutter level? Even when a white teen-aged boy had the temerity to put his hand in my hair, ruffled it and remarked how much like cotton wool it felt, I have to admit that in response I told him in no uncertain terms, including the use of several expletives, never to do it again. I doubt whether he made that mistake again. I've also observed many examples of discrimination in a socioeconomic setting where people of lighter skin colour were consciously given preferential treatment over those of a much darker hue. One only has to look back to even 40 years ago, where upon entering a bank in Barbados, that the front-line staff were predominantly white Barbadians or coffee coloured, and the manager was almost always white or "red-skinned" as they were often referred to.

Older Barbadians who idolise their many famous cricketers will recall that even during the 1950's when the West Indies team dominated the sport, that there existed the racist and humiliating assumption that a black player could not and did not possess the ability to lead, and as a result always had a white captain. It would be 1960 in fact before Sir Frank Worrell became the West Indies first ever black Captain.

I was told by my mother that even my father's parents were somewhat reluctant to allow him to marry her because they considered her to be **"a little too dark"** for their liking and she recounts that they even had a mixed-race woman lined up for him instead, according to her recollection. Much to their annoyance, I understand that they both resisted this attempt to derail their relationship. This type of meddling was one of the reasons which eventually led them to seek a new life in England.

CHAPTER SEVEN

SNOW

My first experience of snow; cold-very cold. When I saw these strange feathery objects fluttering around outside the window, I ran out excitedly to see what they were. White and lovely to behold, the entire ground and rooftops around was covered in this strange stuff. The air was sharp and crisp, and I'll never forget the feeling when I bent down and scooped up a handful of this stuff that looked so much like cotton wool; the outcome was almost immediate and a shock to the senses. To use a commonly uttered oxymoron, the ice burnt like hell. My hands felt as if they were on fire. I quickly shook it off and ran into the house in extreme discomfort to the amusement of my mother.

CHAPTER EIGHT

The Fish and Chip shop and The Secret ingredient

I can still remember the first time we went to a fish and chip shop in Ipswich. The day was cold, crisp, and frosty breath poured from our mouths in white plumes. We screwed up our eyes against the sharp wind as we made our way down the high street to the fish and chip shop. Once inside we rubbed our hands together and stamped our feet to get some feeling back into frozen fingers and toes. To stand in the warmth of the shop queuing was like being transported to heaven. The people in front of us shuffled forward to be served, and eventually it was our turn. Whilst my mum ordered, I gazed up at the man serving and while he scooped the chips out of the sizzling fat, I couldn't help but notice the steady, drip, drip, drip, of clear liquid seeping from his nose and plopping into the fat. Although it was a cold day outside, his sinuses were clearly reacting to the extreme heat as he laboured over the fryers. He was also perspiring profusely which meant that another source of flavouring was inadvertently added to the mixture.

I tugged on mum's hand urgently to draw her attention to the dripping appendage, but she was too engrossed in paying for our supper. She never noticed and I don't remember trying again to tell her as we were more concerned with getting home out of the cold and in front of a warm fire. By the time we had arrived home, I had forgotten what I had noted, and yes, the fish and chips tasted delicious despite the extra ingredient administered by the man frying the fish.

CHAPTER NINE

Stamford Hill

At the age of around ten or eleven, my parents decided to relocate to London after some of the friends they had known in Barbados also migrated to England. They settled in Lower Clapton, a bus ride away from Stamford Hill, which was then and now, known mainly for being a very orthodox Jewish area. People familiar with the area will immediately know of places named, Cazenove Road, Osbaldeston Road, Filey Avenue and others. It was a place of frantic activity, where Jewish men with long curls at the side of their faces and wearing black hats and the furry shtreimel, hurried back and forth conducting their business. I recall young Jewish boys nipping into the salt beef bar or coming out of Grodzinsky, the bakers sometimes running across the busy road and barely making it by the skin of a boot heel. Sometimes called "Little Israel", It was a bleak time for the Jewish community due to the level of anti-Semitic persecution they suffered at the hands of Nazi sympathising fascist groups like the Black Shirts led by Oswald Moseley. Walls and houses were frequently daubed with the anti-Jewish slogan "Juden Rous" or Jews Out. On reflection, here were two groups of people, both despised, reviled and often discriminated against for different reasons, now having to form a symbiotic relationship in order to survive in an extremely hostile environment.

During this period, we resided in turn at first 87 and then 107 Osbaldeston Road. Home became a large single room, with a partition which separated where I slept from my mother and father. There was a well used cooker and a sink in my section. The toilet was outside in the hallway and was a shared facility for all of the tenants in the property which probably numbered around 5 families including ourselves. It wasn't uncommon when the need arose, to try the handle on the door unsuccessfully and hear an impatient voice inside utter the words: **"Somebody's in here!"** It was simply a case of clenching everything, or crossing your legs and waiting till they came out.

Simply through necessity everyone bathed in the same sink they prepared their food in or used a plastic bowl, so a strip wash became the daily norm. The weekly rent for living in these properties would have been around two to five pounds per week but as little as it sounds, it still had to be earned, and with dad still having problems holding down jobs, it fell mainly to Mum to keep bringing in the cash. Our landlords were both Jewish and very orthodox in appearance. Mr. Shingleheim was tall and gaunt with an extremely runny nose which he dabbed constantly ; Mr. Cohen by contrast, was a large portly man who wore glasses with pebble type lenses which made his eyes look as if they would bulge out of his head. Both men though were very quietly spoken and showed great empathy and patience on the frequent occasions when we simply couldn't pay on rent day. Thanks to Mum they always got it eventually. It was either paid from her pay packet or from the money she got from the payout from a "pardner" or partner draw which was a type of syndicate popular amongst West Indians and Africans who called it a "susu".

In these saving clubs, members paid cash in over a set number of months and were then paid out in rotation. The lump sums were used to pay off debts, buy school clothes for children or for eagerly awaited trips back home to visit relatives and friends.

Occasionally in these multiple occupancy houses, there would be minor or even heated disagreements with other tenants, mostly about noise from whoever happened to be living above us at the time. Every time they stomped around too loudly or turned their music up, dad would prod the ceiling with the end of a broom repeatedly until the noise stopped. However, the biggest bone of contention was always about having to wait to use the loo in the hallway or the obvious inconveniences of not having the luxury of one's own bathtub. Eventually, some of us found out about Hackney Baths down in

Lower Clapton at the intersection with Mare Street, where for a shilling or two you could rent a towel and soap and have a wonderful soak in an actual bathtub. I believe they had around ten to fifteen tubs available and sometimes you had to wait quite a long time especially if some folks paid double. It was sheer bliss.

The baths also housed a full-sized swimming pool and although I couldn't swim, the noise of people splashing around in the water was like a magnet, so on one particular occasion I took a pair of swimming shorts with me. After my bath I changed quickly and marched excitedly around to the pool area where upon seeing the wonderfully exhilarating sight of people having fun, I promptly took a running jump and launched myself in the water. Well, how was I to know how deep the water was? I quickly lost control and must have cartwheeled, floundered and spluttered for what seemed an eternity before I felt arms gripping me as a lifeguard fished me out. The experience was so traumatic that it would be another 30 years before I plucked up the courage to venture into another swimming pool, this time for some lessons. To this day, even though I am now far more comfortable in a pool, I treat it and particularly the sea with not only tremendous respect, but still with a little fear.

CHAPTER TEN

Ridley Road Market

Between the ages of eleven and eighteen, and whilst living first in Osbaldeston Road and then latterly Pembury Grove, one of the great features of the locality was Ridley Road Market in Dalston which was a short bus ride away. There you could buy anything from fabrics to records. Most local people went there on a Saturday morning to do their weekend shopping. A bustling, crowded thoroughfare, one could get every type of Caribbean vegetable: Plantain, yams, sweet potatoes and green bananas to name but a few. Many West Indians, I am told, found it difficult at first, adjusting to what came to be described as "English food". My mother once told me that one of her friends had written home to relatives complaining that English people ate "blackened, burnt bread" (toast) and consumed "grass" with their main meals. They would eventually learn that the greenery they described, cress for example, was called salad. It was on one of these weekly expeditions that I soon became aware of some of the more unusual fare available in Ridley Market. On one stall I noticed very large neatly cut chunks of very red meat which had little or no fat on it. This stall was always busy and the vendor was kept occupied first by weighing and then wrapping up the eagerly sought meat for his keen customers. I later found out that this was actually horsemeat which most people insisted that they were buying for their pets, although nowadays we know differently. The few that actually admitted the true purpose for buying it swore that it was the most delicious meat they ever ate. Farther on down the market road, huge boxes swayed very slightly as if something was within. On closer inspection and upon peering inside, one would see that the box was full of huge sea snails with shells twice the size of a mans' fist all undulating as they crawled over each other. Occasionally, a customer would reach into the box, grasp one of these monstrous molluscs and take it into an adjacent lean-to to pay for it. I understand that once purchased, an assistant would prise the "foot" as it was referred to from its shell, slit it open and remove the slime, and then wash and wrap it for the customer. I am told that such snails are a much sought after delicacy amongst West Africans who tell me that one can cost as much as ten pounds in a restaurant. I hasten to add that as I have a morbid fear of even garden snails or slugs, I have always done everything possible to avoid coming into contact with one on a plate or otherwise. Also in this area, one could purchase an entire cooked sheep or just the head if preferred, from a shop at Dalston junction. My father bought a head on quite a few occasions and I always felt a little unnerved looking at the grinning and blackened teeth of the bare skull after the flesh had been stripped off. I know that some people shudder at the thought of eating such fare, but this was the type of food poorer folks bought. In place of margarine we spread white cooking fat on our bread because it was cheap to buy and it was better than eating it dry.

CHAPTER ELEVEN

Dad

It was during this period in the early sixties that I noticed two things about my father. His propensity for handing out a beating and his increasing paranoia. Mum would tell me some years later that before we had come to England, that in a fit of temper, he had pushed a bayonet through the back door of the house whilst in a rage about something. She had run into the house to get away from him and was standing with her back against the door. When the bayonet came through, it was by sheer providence that it only went through the little finger of her left hand severing a tendon in the process. In later years, that finger remained crooked, giving her an appearance of affectation when holding a cup of tea. She also related a story that suggests that he had once said, possibly in a drunken temper that he would prefer me, "the little bastard", dead. I think she really feared for me, but human relationships being what they are, they somehow got past these difficult periods which were always followed by a rather tense stand-off.

Soon after moving to Clapton, dad began to join up with old male friends he used to socialise with in Barbados. They too had migrated to England now and it was clearly time for the pals to regroup. It wasn't long before they would be in the Finsbury Park Tavern, or The Three Crowns in Church Street Stoke Newington. Both of these pubs were notorious for one thing apart from the beer. Prostitutes. Mainly white but not exclusively so as there were lots of black working girls too. Collectively, they not only plied their trade enthusiastically within the ale houses, but also in local roads, one of which was Queens Drive in Haringey where men in cars cruised up and down even in broad daylight, all the while trying to outfox the local constabulary who were eager to move them and the women out of the area. In my late teens and twenties, during my fledgling years as a guitarist, I performed at the Three Crowns and would often see my father and his buddies at play. It was an odd experience to be present at these Friday evening sessions, on one hand trying to concentrate on playing the instrument, whilst at the same time keeping a beady eye on my father from the stage. Men in pubs like these were often accused of either taking their pay packets and blowing it in a local betting shop or paying it straight into the "Hookers Bank" as it was jokingly, if inappropriately termed.

It wasn't uncommon at the end of the evening for people passing to be treated to the unedifying sight of drink-fuelled scuffles breaking out amongst the male patrons as they argued over which of them went off with which prostitute. Thankfully I never actually witnessed my father amongst this group of eager patrons. I believe he was far more discerning and discreet in his own operations.

After a few years, we moved to Pembury Grove, off Clarence Road in Lower Clapton. Living arrangements were much the same as before. Shared single rooms with no proper bathing facilities which meant weekly trips to Hackney Baths for a good scrub and actually, we could now walk down there without needing to catch a bus. Again, noisy neighbours above and dad prodding the ceiling in frustration. As one of only two black families in the street, I often had to endure the taunting from the young male members of two white families that lived across the road from us. Both of the equally obnoxious groups derived enormous pleasure from shouting out offensive comments as me and my school friend, another black lad who lived just down the road, made our way to get the bus to Clapton. The shouting started almost as soon as we appeared. "Wog", "Sambo" and "Blackie" were the most favoured terms of abuse. We endured this behaviour, mainly because the boys were much older and bigger than we were. It's sometimes hard to believe but I can remember bumping into the oldest male around 25 years later, in a pub in Hackney. We recognised each other immediately. We even struck up a brief conversation, during which he actually apologised for the years of misery and fear he had heaped on our young shoulders, trying his best to somehow justify it. I can only imagine that we were probably two of many such victims who had suffered the same torment.

He suggested that we should meet up again for a drink. As I said, it was a brief conversation. I felt like venting the anger that had built up over the years every time I remembered the catcalls from him and his brothers. The words **"Sambo, Wog, Blackie,"** and others reverberated in my head as I looked at his face. I accepted the invitation somewhat hesitantly, but it will come as no surprise when I say that I didn't keep in touch, and that drink never happened.

At this time Mum had decided upon a career in nursing and commenced training at St Leonards hospital in Homerton, whilst also holding down other part-time jobs to make ends meet. Sometimes she would arrive home later as a result. That's when it would start. As I lay in my section of the room, I would hear the accusatory shouts from dad that she had been out with "a man" followed by clump, clump as he held her down and beat her. If I intervened, I got it too. Fists, a kick or two, a leather belt across my legs and back till the welts bled.

In the morning, he would be remorseful to mum asking for forgiveness. Me, he just glared at. How dare I intervene. So when Mum went to work, I got it again. Slaps, punches, the belt. On one occasion because I actually managed to wriggle out of his grasp and ran towards the door to ask for help, he threw a pair of haircutting scissors at me. They actually pierced my right buttock and stuck there as I ran around the room like a human dartboard. I think this shocked even him and he immediately halted his assault and became, inevitably, extremely remorseful. I've still got the two dents in my arse from that night as a permanent reminder.

This was the pattern of our daily living until mum finally had enough and took me to stay with a family she knew in Stoke Newington. By now she had already moved out and was living in nursing quarters while she trained.

During this time on his own, he fell so far behind with payments on the three piece suite, that the bailiffs turned up after repeated County Court warnings. They came to repossess the furniture but he was having none of it, so during the ensuing struggle with a rather large enforcement officer, dad reached over the side of the settee he was pinned down on, grasped a hammer which was lying on the floor and somehow managed to smash the officer over the head with it. The bailiff was badly injured and lost a lot of blood as a result, which led to dad being arrested and spending six months in jail.

Eventually, having been released from prison, he turned up at my school one day and begged me to come home. So, home I went. After all, he must be a changed man surely. Nothing changed. Within days he was grabbing me by the neck, slapping me around the head and shouting at me that it was all my fault that mum had left him. They weren't yet divorced, but I think she never forgave him for his drunken rant one night when she was sleeping in a chair on my side of the room, only to be rudely awakened by him bursting out of the adjoining bedroom brandishing a packet of condoms and shouting:

"Do you see these, you see these? These aren't for you know, these are for someone else!!"

Would any self-respecting woman forgive such a tirade of vulgar abuse? She had been in the habit of still visiting the house on Sundays, mainly for my sake – trying to maintain some semblance of family normality. But now, that stopped altogether. I met her at friends of hers or at hospitals where she worked. My time for leaving would come a little later.

CHAPTER TWELVE

Brooke House

At the age of eleven, I moved to Springfield Junior School in Stamford Hill whilst waiting for a place at Brook House Secondary in Lower Clapton. I can still remember my first day. I recall walking across the grass past the pond, wearing my new uniform and blazer, the outfit completed with a shiny new brown satchel slung over my shoulders. I was in my own little world, when suddenly I hear the pad of feet, quickening now and getting closer. I look around in panic to see around three white lads a little older than myself gaining ground and nearly upon me. Upon reaching me, they force me roughly to the ground, my face pressed into the cold wet grass, pummelling me all the time and uttering crude invectives such as: **"Fucking little coon"** and **"stay down you black bastard",** whenever I tried to get up. Eventually, they would release me and run off laughing. Well, at 11 years old and slightly built, what could I do?

Suffice to say, I was a little messed up when I arrived at the gates of Springfield, jacket and trousers covered in mud, strap from the satchell hanging off.

Dad was really pissed off when I returned home that evening. Out came the belt and yet more welts. It got to a stage where I barely felt any pain from the lashes. Even my body felt numb at times.

Not long after the first Springfield term, I moved to Brook House in Kenninghall Road. From the first year to the fourth, things were pretty much uneventful, but a lot changed in the fifth. The dinner hall was sometimes a somewhat uncomfortable place for us black pupils as we would have to occasionally listen to jibes from a group of white bully boys on a separate table who would recite lewd jokes at us, one of which went like this: **"A white man and a black man were rowing across a lake when suddenly a wave capsized the boat and both occupants were thrown overboard. The white man survived but the black man never reappeared. Do you know why? SHIT DON'T FLOAT!"** as the punch line was delivered, their table would erupt into raucous laughter which would prompt the master on lunch duty to go over and tell them to quiet down. What I mainly recall is that the majority of my black classmates, even at fourteen seemed to be built like brick houses, whilst I remained slight and rather puny looking. By the time they were sixteen, they were all either running for their house teams or playing basketball, cricket or football for the school. The notable pupils in my year were Kenny Johnson and John Isaacs, both of whom were terrific athletes. The two of them excelled at football and athletics. I have to admit I envied and admired both of them in equal measure and wished I had their physical prowess. In fact, the only time I persuaded one of the sports masters to let me represent my house, Kelvin, in a football match against another house, mainly because my house colour was red, the same as Liverpool FC – I had to be carried off with bad grazes after that fool David Edwards, a stocky black kid from Stephenson House sent me flying after 5 minutes! That was the end of my sporting exploits at school.

What marked John out as different, was the fact that, in addition to being black, he was also Jewish the fact of which he often joked about. More than once he would joke: **"As if I didn't have enough problems being black, I had to be bloody Yiddish as well!"** Each morning as the rest of the class filed out and headed for the assembly hall, John would go off in a different direction to a classroom with the rest of the Jewish pupils for his own prayers. He clearly didn't regard either of those characteristics as impediments to his long-term ambitions as he went on to become one of the most highly respected athletics coaches in Britain.

And then there was Herol Burton a brash Jamaican lad who joined our class aged 16, cocky as hell and with a propensity for flashy dressing. In modern day terms he would be described as 'a bit of a dandy' or 'peacock' when it came to his appearance. He wore polka dot shirts with tie pins holding back the collars, cuff links and his trousers had slits at the bottom with little cloth-covered buttons. He was also very proud of his light brown skin and took every opportunity to tease or mock other black lads who had much darker complexions. One such classmate was Wedderburn, a very dark-skinned, unassuming lad. For reasons unknown, apart from stupidity, Burton began referring to him as ***"Blackie", or "You, with the black shiny face!"***

These jibes went on for weeks until such time as Wedderburn had taken as much as he was going to and invited Burton to meet him "and his black shiny face" outside the school gates at 4pm. The classroom rustled with murmurs of excitement at the prospect of a punch up that evening, so it was no surprise to see the huge gathering outside the front of Brooke House later that day.

Wedderburn was the first to arrive accompanied by a few pals and it wasn't too long before Burton pushed his way through to centre of the expectant throng of onlookers of which I was one. Even on this occasion Burton had to be sartorially different and sported a pair of tan driving gloves which, to be honest, looked totally out of place.

After a short period of squaring up to each other, the pair were pushed together by the assembled crowd who were eager to see battle joined. And so it commenced with Burton with his gloved fists up, Queensbury Rules style, poking his left arm out hoping to keep Wedderburn at length for as long as possible. Most of us looking on immediately realized that he was no fighter and it wasn't long before Wedderburn showed that despite his quiet and unassuming manner, he knew how to use his fists. He simply walked through Burton's weak and futile jabs and delivered sickening blow after blow to all parts of his face and head. One could hear the 'thud' and 'clump' sound of each punch. Someone in the baying crowd shouted at Wedderburn to ***"kick him in the nuts man!"*** Wedderburn duly set out to oblige with the request. Burton was game though and even after taking a ferocious, though partially blocked, kick to the groin he refused to be felled. The pavement became more and more blood-spattered with each crunching blow. He staggered and whimpered after each kick or punch connected. We could all see, not only from the tears of pain which seeped from his eyes, but from the array of discoloured swollen bumps increasing around his cheeks and forehead and with the blood dripping from his nose, and split lips. Whenever he winced in pain, one could see his pinkened teeth stained by the blood which leaked from battered gums. After a couple of minutes watching this savage spectacle, some of us rushed in between the two combatants and hauled him away to end his misery. Even a short period of time can feel like an eternity when you're taking a beating. I'm not even sure that Wedderburn actually enjoyed beating Burton that badly. He simply had to defend his honour after being insulted about his appearance, a matter of pride.

And Burton? Apart from never calling Wedderburn "Blackie" again, I guess he took some iota of satisfaction at not being put down, rather like boxer Jake Lamotta following the severe beating he took from Sugar Ray Robinson which ended with Lamotta having been rescued by the referee's intervention, leaning against the blood-soaked ropes, barely able to stand and shouting: ***"you never put me down Ray – you never put me down!"***

I would meet up with Burton many years later as our paths crossed in the world of music.

As for me, in the absence of any athletic prowess whatsoever, I concentrated on literary and artistic subjects and even managed to excel at drawing, painting and English Literature and Language, picking up prizes for portrait drawing and essay writing. Strange how you attract the attention of bullies when you are not only slight of build but seem to achieve a little more than they do. It became almost routine to be tripped in the corridor by Jenkins, Ives, or another member of his gang until one day after one dig in the ribs too many, I challenged him to a punch up in the gym after PE one on one. Obviously he eagerly accepted and after the rest of the pupils had left for the showers, we stood there looking at each other for a while. Eventually he said: **"Well come on then, you c—nt - are we going to look at each other all f—king day?"**, at which point I thought, what the hell and charged at him, threw a punch which clearly took him completely by surprise. He tried in vain to block it but only succeeded in deflecting it straight onto his mouth. I felt my fist connect with his teeth. Jenkins staggered backwards as his mouth began to leak blood. I can still remember the look of shock as he gazed at his blood-stained palm which he had wiped across his split lips. **"You fuckin' cunt – look what you've done!"** Next thing I knew he was striding towards me. I saw his right fist coming towards my face but I was still admiring my own success. As a result, I was totally unprepared. There was a flash of light as the blow caught me high up on the temple. I don't remember falling down but I recall looking up from the floor with Jenkins staring down at me and offering me a hand up. I grasped it, and though a little groggy from the blow, we both left the gym together and made our way to the changing room. To be honest I thought I had got a real break here. Had his two henchmen Ives and Shotton been around, I might have got a real kicking. Just goes to prove that bullies aren't that brave when you get them one on one. Without a word being spoken, we got dressed. He left the gym ahead of me, still nursing his swollen mouth whilst I sat there for a while longer taking in what had just happened. Funny that. I never had any more problems with him. Even though neither one of us had scored an outright victory, it seemed to have earn me a modicum of respect. Did it stop the bullying from others? No. But I then found a way of dealing with it. Every time, Dicks, Ives or Tony Shotton took the piss or gave me a nudge, the answer was simple. There was a little Jewish kid in my class called Barry Rothman. He was even more puny than I was, so every time I took a clout from a bully, he got it from me. Nothing too hurtful, just a pinch, a slap or a sharp rebuke if he annoyed me. This continued for quite some time until Rothman got himself a new pal in the form of Peter Mandelbaum, a huge Jewish kid that joined our class and who became akin to his bodyguard and protector. From then on, every time it looked as though I was about to give Rothman a little prod, Mandelbaum would either glare at me menacingly or get up from his desk and walk over and stand protectively nearby. What a pain in the ass he was.

So what did I do? One day after he stepped in to protect his little friend, he actually grabbed me by the front of my shirt, much to the amusement of the rest of the class. To save face, in a croaky voice, I challenged him to a punch up after school in the gym. Needless to say, he accepted with some relish. I imagine he must already have been visualising himself standing over my inert frame triumphantly.

So there I was, at 4.30 that afternoon jogging into the gym apprehensively, gloved up, wearing a pair of tatty shorts a little big for me and a vest which displayed my under-developed arms. Some excited classmates cheered encouragingly whilst others looked on with glee, already predicting an inevitable outcome. Some of them even shouted out to me with some measure of sarcasm and humour, asking me what kind of flowers I liked.

I was already in the ring for around five minutes, nervously waiting for my opponent to appear, when at last a loud murmur went up around the expectant crowd, and in came Mandelbaum, all togged up as if he was about to fight at Wembley Stadium for the world title. He was resplendent in a gleaming white vest, blue satin shorts and with a matching blue satin gown with white trim draped around his shoulders. I must admit he looked the part and I looked a right idiot.

When he entered the ring, Mr Prosser, our games master, called us to the centre and gave us the usual spiel about "having a nice clean fight" and "protect yourselves at all time" etc. Yeah right, as if that was ever going to happen.

We touched gloves, returned to our respective corners and at the sound of the bell approached each other at first warily, but after about a minute of meaningless feinting and jabbing at each other without actually landing any punches (much to the displeasure of the assembled throng ringside who wanted to see blood spilled), Mandelbaum suddenly became impatient and rushed at me and aimed a right swing at my head.

"If you're going to land anything on the lanky fucker, it's going to have to be now", I thought. Being around eight inches shorter than him, it wasn't that hard to duck down under the swinging arm, move inside and bring my head upwards. Flush on his nose.

I heard him grunt in pain and then suddenly, his vest wasn't so white anymore as blood sprayed from the damaged appendage and soaked the material. He staggered backwards and seeing my chance, I rushed in wildly swinging punches at his head, many of which missed, but it was enough to force him back onto the ropes and cover up as best as he could.

That was enough for Mr Prosser who leapt in, pulled me off and raised my hand as the winner. Imagine that. Little me, a winner in a scrap.

Some wild cheering along with a little laughter broke out around the ring as I ducked through the ropes and made my way out to the changing rooms, leaving the vanquished Mandelbaum sitting on his stool having his nose patched up.

I never had any more trouble from him again. And to think of it, Barry Rothman never had any from me because this cathartic moment imbued me with a new found confidence. I like to think that even the bully boys, Jenkins, Shotton and Ives seemed to view me differently.

This was indeed a good day.

CHAPTER THIRTEEN

The Park

Hanging out with the lads as a teenager meant mainly two things:

One was partying at the weekend, or meeting up in Downs Park, Lower Clapton, to play football, cricket or to check out the local girls. It was a place where, If you chatted to someone else's girl, the boyfriend would come up to and kick you in your face while you lay on the grass sunning yourself. The black boys regarded this Park as their domain: a place where friendships were forged, fights were fought and reputations made or dashed.

The Park was the place where teenaged boys tested the patience of the eagle-eyed park keepers by playing grass destroying football matches on the pristine surface of the crown bowling green. At least until the cry of ***"Watch out – Parkie's coming!".*** Upon hearing this warning, and with the park keeper approaching at a frantic pace, the ball was picked up and all present would run off as fast as they could, leaving the previously carpet-like covering of grass full of scuffs and deep gouges.

The nearby districts of Dalston, Stoke Newington and Shoreditch were regarded as the mean streets, where we joked that even stray cats and dogs only went around in pairs.

The Park was where two local guys, Billy and Bredda In law strutted through wearing tight jeans and string vests to show off their physiques. Most of us looked on the two of them with a mixture of respect, envy and fear. None of us knew (or dared to ask) how Bredda In law got his nickname.

This was also the scene of some of the most vicious beatings handed out by one West Indian teenager to another as shouts of encouragement were bellowed excitedly by the frenzied crowd surrounding the two combatants, as blood sprayed around the throng and dappled the grass. On occasion the one coming off worse and having had enough would turn tail and try to break through the baying mob, only to be grabbed and pushed back into the fray to be battered some more until at last, mercifully, a passer-by or a park keeper would intervene and haul the loser, who by now could barely stand up, away.

Downs Park was the place where Bunny Braithwaite had his teeth rearranged. His name was actually Colin, but was given the nickname "bunny" on account of his two front teeth which protruded slightly below his upper lip, giving him a somewhat leporid or rabbit-like appearance.

Rumour had it that he had made unwanted advances to some girl at a party and the news got back to her boyfriend. A few days later, Bunny was lying on the grass in the park watching a cricket match between two local teams. He was so engrossed with the sound of leather on willow or on parts of the batsman's body as the fast bowler delivered each ball with bad intent, that he totally failed to notice the approach of the wronged boyfriend.

Without uttering a word, the protagonist strode up to Bunny and gave him a ferocious kick to the left side of his face, splintering mandibles and teeth in a welter of shattered bone and blood. He then turned and walked off leaving the unconscious would be lover-boy twitching on the ground. Bunny spent a month in the hospital and eventually returned to school with his face wired together and still pretty swollen. He got little sympathy from the other guys in his 6th form group. Well, everyone knew that if you risked chatting to another guy's girl and got found out, the outcome would either be a beating or even worse, you could even end up getting slashed across the face and scarred for life. These were pretty dangerous and risky times for a black youth growing up around Hackney and you had to, not only watch your back but also try to surround yourself with some guys who could handle themselves. If you weren't any good at fighting you had to be able to run pretty damn fast.

We all looked forward to the weekend and finding out where the blues party was on Saturday night which meant dressing up in a swanky mohair suit, Fred Perry shirt, fancy shoes which were often a size too small, and not forgetting a silk hankie tucked into the breast pocket of the jacket. Finding a blues party wasn't difficult. If you hadn't been invited to one, it was simply a matter of trawling the local streets of St Marks Rise in Dalston or Downs Park Road, listening for the thudding bass of a sound system or looking to see in which direction any similar groups of would be revellers were heading.

The one major risk attached to randomly walking into any party uninvited was that it might be a party where Frank and Mike Grant happened to be. They were two of three brothers who had a fearsome reputation locally. Oddly enough, the youngest of the three, Dennis, went to the same school as I in Hackney and was a very likeable and mild-mannered teenager. He actually boxed for the school and as far as we knew only handed out beatings in the ring, unlike his two older siblings who would mete out severe retribution to anyone who committed the slightest misdemeanour such as treading on their expensive shoes or bumping into them a little too boisterously. If you went to any party and saw the Grants there, you left promptly before bottles or fists began flying all over the goddamn place.

And then there were the Benn brothers. I recall that whenever I turned up at their home, the oldest brother Timothy, nicknamed Porky, would look at me suspiciously. He fancied himself as a bit of a ladies' man although in truth, it was rumoured that most recently he had bedded a woman whose ardour was so hard to quench that poor Porky had to resort to subterfuge in order to escape from the bedroom with some dignity and his reputation still intact. We hear that he complained that "the damn woman just wouldn't go to sleep! Apparently, after nearly 2 hours of being gripped fiercely about the loins by this insatiable nymphomaniac, he looked down at her only to see her giving him a look which seemed to say: ***"Is that all you got?",*** at which point he managed to somehow extricate himself, feign cramp in a hamstring and make a hasty escape from the bed. Porky remarked that it was if she 'wanted to kill him with it!'

The truth was, the young men of the day really had to be on their mettle when it came to bedroom romps with such sassy young women. You could be sure that within 24 hours of leaving the sheets, every one of their friends would have had a report on not only one's performance, but also a rating and detailed description of one's manhood including its length and girth, or indeed the lack of.

So here was Porky, looking at me quizzically and asking: ***"And what are you guys going to be getting up to tonight – hoping to get lucky?*** with a nudge and a wink.

The real problem here wasn't getting lucky, but returning home with your brand new silk hankie intact as someone usually whipped it out of your pocket when you weren't looking. Most of us took the precaution of using a common pin to secure it in place, that way at least you would feel a tug as the would-be thief tried his luck. Whenever this happened, there would be a commotion as the cry of **"What the hell are you doing man?"** went up and an exchange of words or at worst a minor scuffle would ensue.

Samuel, the middle brother was a tall gangly lad with a reputation for being very studious. He was determined to go on to university to study economics or business. He and I were great friends and spent a lot of social time together. The youngest of the trio, Henry, was a cocky seventeen year old who was forever breaking up and getting back with his girlfriend Paula, a pretty local girl from Lower Clapton. Every time the two of them had a row and split up, there was a mad scramble from many of the guys in the area, keen to replace him which caused a great deal of paranoia in poor Henry's head.

It was also pretty dangerous to be seen chatting to Paula even innocently as I found out to my cost.

I had bumped into her by chance while walking through Downs Park one afternoon and we were exchanging idle gossip and chatter when one of Henry's cronies, named Danny, happened to walk past us while we were talking. I remember him glancing at us suspiciously before hurrying by without even saying **"Hi"** as you would expect. Later that evening I was at home when I heard someone tapping on the glass of our front room window.

Drawing back the curtain and peering out I could see Henry standing on the top step by the front door looking somewhat agitated.

I went out, opened the door and before I could say hello he was in my face, eyes bulging and looking as if he could kill.

Drawing back the jacket he was wearing with his right hand, he revealed a knife tucked into a sheath worn on his belt.

"I come to cut yuh," he hissed at me punctuating the threat with several choice expletives. **"Someone tell me yuh been chatting to Paula!"**

Well, it didn't take too much effort to figure out that the "someone" must have been that rat Danny. Before I could even try to explain, he made to draw the knife. Luckily for me, at that precise moment, my Dad appeared behind me and asked: **"And what are you two plotting now? Up to no good I expect, eh Henry?"**

Henry quickly closed his jacket, concealing the knife before muttering: **"No**

Sir. Just talking to Jay about a party we're going to at the weekend".

Dad replied: **Well don't keep him out here too long – he's got things to do, okay?"** Then he turned and was gone as suddenly as he had fortuitously appeared.

Henry said: **"You're f-----g lucky yu father come out. Listen. Don't ever talk to Paula again, about anything. Don't even say hello to her, yu understand?"**

I nodded in affirmation. Then he was gone.

"Phew!" I thought to myself. That was too close. But that was Henry for you. Extremely paranoid, teetering on the edge and seeing every other male in the area as a potential threat.

His paranoia was no doubt brought on by a somewhat traumatic experience from a couple of years back when the bunch of guys he was hanging out with invited him around to one of the other lad's homes for a daytime 'session'. He eagerly accepted thinking it was for a drink up, some male bonding and a few laughs.

Suffice to say that he got rather a nasty surprise upon arrival to find that the 'session' planned was of the fleshy kind, the lads having coerced a local girl they knew, around to the house, and they were all planning to take turns in the bedroom. At some point, after a few had gone in and emerged grinning, Henry was pushed towards the bedroom. Upon entering, the blood drained from all parts of his frame however when he saw that the girl in the room was none other than his then girlfriend spread out like a butterfly on the bed.

He croaked ***"what the F—ck?"***

And she uttered ***"Shit! Henry!"***, pulling the sheets up to hide her nakedness as Henry turned and ran from the room and made straight for the door of the house, with the sound of hysterical laughter from the other guys ringing in his ears as he went.

Another guy who arrived at the house later to join in the "session" said he had passed Henry on the way. Bajie, as he was known, due to his pronounced, lilting, Barbadian accent recounted his brief encounter with the fleeing Henry, saying: "I saw the man coming towards me, so I called out to him, but he just rushed past me walking fast, as though he'd seen a ghost!"

Henry never spoke to those guys or the girl again. Well, they do say that if you lay down with dogs, there's a good chance that you'll get fleas.

The highlight of the Saturday night party would be finding your own cosy spot with your back against a wall, where you could drink a Cherry B or two and with luck find a girl to smooch with. Often one had to settle for just the drink and you left the party smooch-less, but either slightly drunk or fuzzy brained after breathing in the smoke from the weed being smoked. I recall that although none of us could drive at that age, we somehow always managed to find a party that was within walking distance or a short bus ride from our homes, anywhere around Dalston or Clapton.

Apart from Henry and Samuel, I also hung out with some other local guys, Gossip, (so called because you couldn't tell him anything without it being broadcast to everyone), TC and another simply called H. The latter named, was at 17 a confident guitar player and was already touring with well established recording artists. Like me, H was Barbadian by birth and at that stage my interest in guitars was becoming quite obsessive, especially as Jimi Hendrix had recently exploded onto the music scene. We couldn't believe that a black man could play music like that. H was already bitten by the Hendrix bug and could already play Purple Haze note for note, and even play the guitar with his teeth and holding the damn guitar behind his head. What a show off I used to think enviously.

One afternoon, Gossip, TC, H and myself were out and about strolling along Stoke Newington High Road, when H caught sight of a rather pretty girl standing on the pavement outside a betting shop. Some guys never learn, do they? Only a week earlier, TC had gone through the unfortunate though self-inflicted experience of having been disturbed in the wrong bed, in the wrong house, and had to exit the property at pace through a window clutching his clothes in his hands and leaving his shoes behind. And now we have H, breaking into what is nowadays best described as a "gangster limp" rude boy style, having decided to try his luck with this girl. He was only around thirty seconds into his chatting up routine when an immensely muscled figure appeared in the doorway of the betting shop.

Bredda In law took in the scene and launched himself into action.

Gossip called out to the busy Lothario who was by now otherwise engaged and oblivious to the impending danger.

Too late. It only took Bredda In Law a few strides to reach H, grab him by his shoulder, spin him around and deliver a sickeningly ferocious punch to the left side of his jaw which lifted him off the ground and propelled him backwards to end up sprawled in a crumpled heap on the pavement. Bredda In law approached the inert form and leaned over the inert form of H, but it was clear he was out cold. He took his girlfriend roughly by the arm and marched her away, only turning once to give us a menacing glare. What did we do?

Did we run after him, confront him and have a go? after all, there were still three of us. Really? This was Bredda In law, the man mountain for Christ sake. For all we knew, his equally huge side-kick Billy was more than likely nearby so it was utterly out of the question. Besides, while H was pretty athletic and of stocky build, the other three of us were rather puny or spindly, and probably incapable of fighting our way in to OR out of a paper bag. Therefore, discretion being the better part of valour, or cowardice actually, we waited until he was out of sight and then hurriedly ran over to H, helped him to his feet and accompanied him to his house to tend to his now swollen face. Luckily the jaw wasn't broken but a few teeth were definitely loosened on that unfortunate day. For many weeks after the incident, Poor H had to suffer jibes like: **"Hey H. I hear Bredda In Law give yuh a slap in yuh mout' for chattin' to his woman!".** Well, H eventually had the last laugh on all of us as he went on to forge an enviable career as an award- winning guitarist and producer.

We never did find out why Bredda In Law was so called. We guessed that he had to be someone's brother in law but we certainly weren't going to ask him.

CHAPTER FOURTEEN

Changes

After leaving Brook House at 18 I attended East Ham Technical college having enrolled for a fine arts course. I recall some of the fellow students that linger on in my memory. There was "Nose Drinker" as we all called him. He was given this nickname because of his long beaky nose which had the unfortunate habit of always becoming immersed in whatever vessel he was drinking out of ; cup of tea or glass of coke, his nose always got in the way. In the end, the only way to prevent this dip, he only half filled his cup or glass. The stand out couple in the art group were Jeff Kench and Allannah Hamilton, an extremely photogenic couple who looked as though they had both dropped out of the pages of a magazine. Needless to say, because of their looks, they were either liked or despised in equal measure. Then there was Manny, a Jewish guy from Stamford Hill whom I used to travel to college with on the bus from Hackney to East Ham. Sometimes I used to hang out after college at his house in the evenings. We had a major falling out over a rather attractive girl in our tutorial group. He, like many of the other lads in the art group was always going on about wanting to date her. One afternoon he and I were sitting in the college café when he announced to the entire table that he had asked her out and she had said okay. Well, me and my big mouth: **"What, is she desperate then?"** I joked. To my surprise, the dumb prick slung the plastic cup of orange he was drinking in my face. My response was to reach across the table we were at, grab him by his shirt and deliver a punch which sent him flying backwards into the person sitting directly behind. I got up, leaving him sprawled on the floor, brushed past the others at the table and made my way to the lift. As the lift doors were closing, I heard a commotion outside which told me that Manny was up and trying to catch up with me. He didn't make it in time so I managed to get to the 4th floor and had long arrived at the classroom when Manny burst in. I heard someone shout, **"Look out!"** I turned around, just in time to see a bloody faced Manny charging towards me with a large T-square. I only just managed to grab the hand with the weapon in it and stopped him in his tracks. It was clear he wanted to do some damage, and I could have decked him again, but his very bloody face told me I had done enough, so there we stood, both gripping each other by the neck grunting and panting. We were eventually separated by some other classmates and kept apart until a tutor arrived and gave us a severe reprimand and a warning about our future behaviour. And that was the end of that friendship. Well, the schmuck did try to take my head off. We never spoke again and did everything possible to avoid each other both at tutorials and away from them and neither of us ever actually dated the young woman. I left after one term because I failed to get a grant for a second, but worse than that, dad ripped up all of my terms work in a temper. Every drawing, painting and sketch was trashed. So that was that. No career as an illustrator or graphic design for me then. Dad just told me to **"get out there and find a fucking job".**

And so the game of job hunting began and it wasn't long before I realised this was not going to be easy. It became routine for me to phone for a job advertised and be invited for an interview, only to be met by: **"Oh. Was it you that rang up? I'm so sorry but the job went some time ago".** My very English accent led all potential employers to think I was white on the phone, only for them to recoil in utter bewilderment when they saw my brown face.

On and on this went until I was eventually hired by the Metal Box Company in Urswick Road Hackney as a machine operator, or so I thought. The morning I turned up and reported to the foreman, I expected to be sat at a bench or machine to do a hands-on job. Instead, he said **"You see that broom over there? Take it and sweep all the trash and metal filings from the floor!"** So that's what I did for most of the day. When I wasn't sweeping around peoples feet, at the end of the day I went around with a bin collecting all of the irregular shaped tins that were unfit for use. I would then sit and cut them up with a larger pincer, toss them in the bin and drag this out to a skip. This was bloody and agonising work as the jagged tins shredded my fingers so needless to say, I left this job after only a week. Not a great start at all. I figured that things had to get better soon. Didn't they?

CHAPTER FIFTEEN

Strange goings on in Barley Lane

So here I was. My plans for a career in which I could put my talent for illustrating in absolute tatters, finding it virtually impossible to find suitable work because of my brown face and desperate to find anything that would take me out of that difficult home environment. By now, Dad wasn't hitting me anymore. That stopped a short while back when he walked into the room one evening holding a leather belt to give me another thrashing when, to his surprise I said: **"If you hit me with that, it'll be the last thing you do!"** His response was to utter a laugh of disbelief and to approach me anyway with what I determined was the usual bad intentions, so when he reached out to grab my shoulder, I slipped inside his outstretched arm, grabbed him by the front of his shirt and slammed him against a wall. I was past caring. He would have had to kill me this time. Luckily for me, dad wasn't a large man, so, slight as I still was, the element of surprise paid dividends. My face must have been some picture: **"But look at this boy - Yuh attacking your father now eh? Yuh think yuh too big now eh?"** he rasped through a slightly hoarse voice now as I continued to force him against the wall with my right hand curled into a fist ready to hit him very hard if he resumed his onslaught. He didn't. As I released my grip on his shirt, he stepped away from me and slunk off into the adjoining room only pausing once to turn and glare at me. And that was that. He never hit me again, although I'm sure it probably crossed his mind on several occasions.

Not long after my emancipation from the lash of the belt and with a new sense of confidence, I decided to try my hand at something completely different, so I applied to Goodmayes Hospital in Essex to train as a psychiatric attendant. I felt that in addition to getting me away from home that it would allow me use a completely new set of skills.

I was right. I took to it like a duck to water and found it strangely fascinating, given that many of the patients were deemed to be quite dangerous. Due to the unpredictable behaviour of many of the inhabitants, it was essential for the staff to count the cutlery before and after serving meals in case an item was stashed away for later use. Many of the wards at Goodmayes were locked, so it was essential to count the patients at the start and end of each shift. Despite a regimental procedure of keeping tabs on those most likely to abscond, one or two somehow managed to slip past us.

Oliver was such an escape artist. On one occasion after searching all of the hospital premises and the grounds for him to no avail, we eventually received a phone call from a greengrocers shop in the town centre. The caller said: ***"I think we've got one of yours here. Can you come down asap and collect him please?"***

Three of us jumped into a car and made our way into town. Our arrival must have looked like a scene out of a Jack Nicholson movie when we leapt out the car dressed in our white coats and rushed into the shop. It was quite a surreal sight that greeted us: The staff and three or four customers were all huddled together behind the counter looking rather apprehensive whilst Oliver stood virtually still in the centre of the shop eating as many bananas as he could. Several discarded skins lay at his feet. We gently coaxed him from the premises, leaving the relieved staff and shoppers to resume their business.

Besides being a rather adept absconder, Oliver, had another less savoury party piece, which was to sit on his bed and wait until the ward was packed with visitors, at which time he would remove his pyjama bottoms, expose himself and begin a very public and vigorous bout of onanism in full view of all and sundry. The staff would usually be alerted by screams or shouts of revulsion from shocked visitors and staff would have to run over to Oliver's bed and cover him up before removing him to another part of the ward behind a screen, all the while apologising profusely and keep him there until visiting time had ended.

Other patients had other peculiar habits: One pulled a gangrenous little toe off in the night. I recall walking onto the ward one morning and another staff member calling out: **"Hey,– come and have a look at this!"** I went over to my colleague who was standing by the bed of the patient named George – the sheets were pulled back and there on the bed was the blackened digit just lying there. George obviously felt no discomfort and actually looked rather pleased with himself. Another patient had a vile habit of pressing his bell for attention, and when a staff member went over to him, he would ask him to bend closer so that he could whisper something to him. As the unsuspecting attendant leaned over to him, he would then regurgitate the entire contents of his stomach into the attendant's face coating it in vomit. I know because he did it to me. He caught me totally by surprised when I bent down with my ear close to his mouth. Without warning, he belched and gave me a good quantity of his stomach contents full in the face, some of which ended up in my mouth as I gasped and gagged. Bits of carrot, meat, gravy, the lot, I got it all. To add insult to injury, as I recoiled, using my fingers to wipe the muck from my face, he shouted through gritted teeth: ***"Now fuck off back to monkeyland!"***

He only caught me out once with the regurgitated free meal, but such comments were commonplace, as he hurled insults of one type or another at all of the staff though mine had a racial element to it.

Another patient, having taken a liking to certain members of staff, and viewing them as particularly worthy of a "special" gift, would on occasions, call them over and then present them with a handful of Maltesers sized, perfectly spherical balls of faecal matter which he had sculpted secretly and somehow managed to hide them from view for days until they had hardened.

Apart from these daily incidents, which was accepted as part of the job, one of the more unpleasant but necessary duties was to perform the "last offices" on newly deceased patients. I was tasked with washing and shaving the body as well as stuffing the orifices with gauze to prevent body fluids from leaking out before it could be wheeled on a trolley to the morgue and placed in the refrigerator. Funny to think that inevitably, we all end of in cold storage with only a tag attached to our foot to distinguish us from the cadaver on the shelf above.

Suffice to say that the two years spent at Goodmayes was a challenging experience somewhat tempered by an extremely active and excessive social life which consisted of basically one wild party at the nurses home after another, drunken brawls and frantic, debauched bed-hopping. Males resided on the ground floor with the females on the upper floor, and frequent spot checks were carried out by the resident wardens to keep the hankie-pankie to a minimum. It was rumoured that one always had to be prepared to dive into a wardrobe at any moment while one was "visiting". Many of the guys would wait until as late as possible after lights had gone out around 11pm before meeting up with their mates to begin what was called a reconnaissance mission. This consisted of creeping along the darkened female corridor and looking for the door of ones chosen paramour with the aid of a torch. If a key was left in the lock outside, it was mission accomplished although one had to be mindful not to leave the key in the door once inside. A few of them said that It wasn't unusual to be "in the nest" for the night, and having forgotten to remove the key, when the door would be thrust open and in would step another Romeo with lusty intent who would then say **"oops!, Sorry!"** and make a hasty withdrawal although not the entry or withdrawal he originally had in mind. During this time, it was often hard to fathom who was actually going out with whom. In my case, it was many months before I discovered that the female I considered to be my "girlfriend" had not only been meeting up with a married man once a week in a country lane, but she was also engaged in "an arrangement" with one of the hospital caretakers long before I had even arrived. A hard lesson indeed for a "Freshie" like me from North London to learn about human relationships where the female of the species is concerned. I immediately gave her the boot, even though it was apparent that she clearly would have preferred to maintain the status quo, so to speak. It was a period of such alcoholic and social excess that it was bound to end badly, and suddenly at the "Bedhoppers Hotel" as the home was nicknamed. And it did.

Even though I was barely 20 years of age, I socialized with a mixed group of males, some Mauritian, others English and a couple of Chinese guys aged 25 to 30 who also lived in at the hospital. After a rather boozy weekend which had culminated in attending a dance at King Georges hospital in Ilford, I had a minor argument with one of them named Jacques, who was ironically my closest friend at the time. It was something stupid over some records lent to one of his previous girl-friends which I wanted back I think that during the heated exchange of words I called the girl a slut and he called me a fucking idiot!

We were both on duty on the same ward the next morning and during the night I had gone over the entire scenario over and over again and by the time morning came, I was seething having convinced myself with the aid of more alcohol that I wasn't happy with his attitude.

I remember walking onto the ward that morning and as fate would have it, the first person I saw was – Jacques. ***"Hey! I want a word with you!"*** I shouted at him. Well – before we knew it, we had rushed at each other and had grabbed each other first by the scruff of our white coats, then we were rolling on the floor of the ward grappling and grunting. By now we were surrounded by an excited ring of patients urging us on. It felt like ages, but in real time it must have been a couple of minutes before the crowd of patients parted and we were separated, hauled to our feet by some other staff members and marched to the Seniors office and given such a dressing down that it culminated in Jacques getting a severe reprimand as he was in the final year of his training and me being dismissed. And that was the end of an interesting period of my early life and a great friendship which was never repaired.

Having been unceremoniously thrown out of Goodmayes Hospital, and having been given a months' notice during which I had to find somewhere to live, I encountered similar obstacles as in my early teens. My accent got me many appointments but the places were "just gone" whenever I turned up to view the room or flat. It was always the same when they saw the brown face. In the end and, by now desperate to avoid wasting my time, I started saying to prospective landlords: "Oh by the way, I should mention that I'm black! – Is that going to be a problem?" In many cases it was, but at least this approach sorted the wheat from the chaff so to speak, and I eventually struck lucky and found a place in Margery Park Road, Forest Gate, East London.

I can still recall the feeling of emptiness as I got into the taxi with my few belongings. Not only had I been ignominiously dismissed from a job I liked a lot, but here I was heading off into the unknown. Several years later I would buy an album titled "Cracked Rear View" and looking back now, that precisely described the situation I was in. Looking out of the back of that cab and seeing everything disappearing into the distance was like viewing everything through a broken rear view mirror.

Many months later I visited Goodmayes and Jacques, but it was a mistake. Our conversation was somewhat frosty and it proved to be too difficult to put the past behind us. The friendship had been damaged beyond repair. For many years after, I'm not ashamed to admit I felt that loss, caused by the impetuosity of youth and perhaps a little arrogance. To be honest, I missed his friendship with deeper regret than I would have admitted, but I also knew I had to move on as he had clearly done. As they say – it isn't possible to warm yourself in yesterdays sunshine.

CHAPTER SIXTEEN

Helter Skelter

My new abode in Margery Park turned out to be a 2-roomed split level flat, sparsely furnished but in good order and close to bus and train routes which was really convenient as I had managed to get a new job working at Gamages, a department store in Holborn.

The year spent at this address was eventful, to say the least. I was situated on the upper floor of the property, above two very pleasant young English guys in their mid-twenties who appeared to work from home and were clearly not short of money. Malcolm and Tony, both drove sporty cars and dressed well. They were also extremely chatty and pleasant and within a few months, I was being invited to some interesting parties with wine flowing and many other substances on offer.

It took me a few more months to realize, mainly through the steady flow of visitors to the apartment below that they weren't friends visiting but customers.

During this period of time, several things occurred.

Many people were now listening to drug-inspired music by Hendrix, King Crimson and Pink Floyd and with my interest in guitar playing at a peak, I was further inspired by newly found friends in the area, both black and white. I met Pete Andrews, a black guy who modelled his appearance on Jimi Hendrix and played in a local band. One or two members of the then up and coming Supertramp who were friends of Pete would visit my flat now and then. The two members from a band called Clark –Hutchinson also used to come around with acoustic guitars and there would be weekly jam sessions with other visitors turning up and joining in with the revelry. I'm not sure how much the neighbours enjoyed these noisy get-togethers. Fashion wise, these hippy types all wore bell bottomed pants and long military coats purchased from the local Army surplus stores, and wore their hair long. I found myself enmeshed in a world of psychedelia and music scenes where LSD was openly taken and even I experimented on one occasion, more out of curiosity than anything. This was a strange, new world full of amazing hallucinations and wild imaginings and to be honest, I found it rather scary. This so called 'mind-expanding' drug is widely believed to have been the source of inspiration for many of the Beatles' materials such as 'Strawberry Fields', 'Lucy in the sky with Diamonds' and 'I am the Walrus'.

LSD was taken on small squares of blotting paper which was chewed and swallowed or in tablet form. It usually took around 15 to 30 minutes before one felt any effect and then the room you were in with friends, also tripping, would suddenly be transformed into a world of crazy colours and sounds. Those who indulged in this particular hallucinogenic drug always ensured that there was at least one sober person present in case the drug made them do something daft. Many were aware that in America it had been reported on more than one occasion that some people under its influence had got the notion that they could even fly. Having taken off from a high window ledge, they all discovered that this was indeed a fantasy, after landing with a splat on someone's car or the pavement below.

The Amphetamine contained in the LSD played havoc with one's body clock and kept you awake for hours, but the after effects resulted in you sleeping for a very long time to recover. To be honest, once was enough for me as I didn't even enjoy smoking grass as it only sent me to sleep and it soon became evident to others that I wasn't a very good hippy.

In essence, this was a period of crazy excess which at first I found to be strangely exciting, and through it all I managed somehow to keep my job in Holborn completely on track, never missing even a single day. Things moved at an extremely fast and frenetic pace during this period during which many things happened, and not all of them good.

For one, I came very close to death once after unwittingly being gassed whilst having a bath one day. I had taken the day off and had decided to have a long, slow soak before going out. I had only been laying in the bathtub for around ten minutes or so when I began to feel rather drowsy after trying to sit up a couple of times. I found myself slipping further and further down into the bathtub. I tried to call out for help but my voice only came out in a croak. I began to panic slightly and in desperation reached behind me for something with which to bang on the bathroom door which was adjacent to my left shoulder. By sheer providence, I somehow managed to reach over the edge of the bath and bang loudly on the door. Fortunately for me, Malcolm's girlfriend was in, heard the banging and rushed up to my flat. Later I learned that she had then gone out to the street and asked a man passing by to come and help kick the flat door open, push open the door of the bathroom and haul me semi-conscious from the tub. The ambulance was called and I was rushed to the nearest hospital and revived with oxygen. In cat terms, I must have been down to around seven lives. Even though I had been fortunate enough to have cheated death, when I returned home and had time to fully comprehend what had occurred, I was quite mortified at having been hauled completely naked from a bathtub, thereby displaying my genitals to all and sundry. Despite this brief spell of negativity, I was very grateful indeed to have survived. This cat with a diminished number of lives had so nearly become a dead duck.

It turned out that the old Ascot water heater was leaking gas very slowly and had the bathroom window not been slightly open it may well have been curtains for me, no pun intended.

And then there was the creaky floorboard in the bedroom which drove me to distraction for months. From day one, every time I walked across a particular part of the room, it would make the most annoying sound until one day I'd had enough and decided to nail it down if necessary, anything to stop the damn noise.

Moving a table out of the way, I hauled the thin piece of carpet back to reveal the offending slat of wood and immediately noticed how worn it looked around the ends

– almost as if it had been levered back and replaced on some occasion.

Arming myself with a sturdy screwdriver, I inserted it into one end of the floorboard and with very little effort managed to lift up the end and pull it up and away revealing the cavity below. It was only a few moments before I noticed a fairly large package in clear plastic wrapping. I lifted out the package, which seemed to weigh quite a bit, and took it over to the table and removed the outer covering which then revealed a tin foil inner wrapping. Inside the inner covering was a large block of dark resin like material which I leant forward and sniffed. Yup, I thought to myself. Well I'll be damned if this isn't someone's stash of Black Leb or Lebanese cannabis. It definitely wasn't Red Leb or Acapulco Gold, or even weed.

I replaced the floorboard, secured it firmly with a few nails and, satisfied that the creaking problem was eliminated, replaced the carpet. It didn't take me too long to figure out what to do with my discovery.

That evening I called Tony up from downstairs and showed him the stash which was clearly of no interest to me. He nearly did somersaults. "Do you know how much this shit would cost me from my supplier in Kensington Market? Over a fuckin grand!". I told him to make me an offer, which he did and I gladly accepted 300 pounds cash for what had clearly been hidden and forgotten by a previous occupant of the apartment.

And that was the beginning and the end of my short and unplanned career in cannabis supplying.

During this time I also met a couple of Asian guys from East Ham named Locky and Errol and sometimes they would come around and play cards till late. The former was a gregarious, outgoing character always quick with a funny remark while Errol was more subdued, of slender build and with eyes that darted around which gave him a rather shifty demeanour. He is best remembered for comments he often made about his love of going up to young women and "pressing" their breasts, as he described it, together with his apparent liking for squeezing himself up against unsuspecting women on very crowded trains and remaining insitu until they got off, even if it meant him going past his own stop. He was probably the type of pond life who referred to women as "tail" or "a piece of ass" like another nauseous individual whom I would have the misfortune to acquaint briefly in coming years. Errol was a real sleazebag in short, and I had the impression that he was the type to keep an eye on. And I wasn't wrong in that assessment.

My 21st birthday arrived and went without too much event but what was particularly significant was the discovery upon arriving home from work, was that during the day my Mom had been around and left me a present. I remember opening the door of my flat and seeing this quite large parcel which had been placed on the chest of drawers in the living room. I unwrapped it hastily and was heartened to discover that she had bought me a Portadyne tape recorder upon which she had left me a message wishing me a happy birthday and saying she hoped to see me at the weekend. I was so thrilled with this that I don't believe I actually ever recorded anything on the player for fear of erasing mum's words.

I valued it that much and played it over and over again.

The following evening, Locky and Errol came around to play cards and have a few drinks. Well, actually more than a few drinks. I can remember Locky leaving around midnight but continued playing cards with Errol until eventually I must have fallen asleep or passed out more likely in an alcoholic stupor. When I awoke it must have been gone 3 or 4 in the morning and I was alone. Clearly Errol had gone after I had flaked out so I didn't even go down to the lower floor but turned in to call it a night.

Most of us will recall a moment when you walk through a room and somehow feel that it looks different but just can't put your finger on why. I actually went to work the next day and didn't give it another thought. It wasn't until I arrived home in the evening that I realized what was different about the room – the tape recorder was missing!

My mind went into overdrive. What wicked bastard had stolen it? What sort of lowlife would do such a thing? Well, I had two in mind. The next day I phoned Locky and told him about the missing item. I asked him if he thought Errol could have stolen it, bearing in mind that he was the last to leave the night before. He said he could not believe that Errol could have done it. He just wasn't that type of person.

The next day, decided to do some of my own detective work. I went to the local High Street in East Ham and eventually arrived outside the second-hand shop. Well, knock me down with a feather if my tape recorder wasn't sitting there in the shop window at a knock down price.

I rushed into the shop, my hopes high, and approached the man who owned it with my heart almost bursting out of my chest. I asked him when the recorder was brought in and he described to a tee, the person and the day it came in to see him. His description came as no surprise. I explained the circumstances which had brought me to the shop and had high hopes that he was going to let me take it away. That would have been the end of it. But he refused, and who can blame him? He didn't know me from Adam and had clearly paid the person a sum of money for it. It was now down to me to take the matter to the police or into my own hands.

I left the second-hand shop rather deflated, all the while thinking: ***"When I see that Errol, boy, am I gonna kick his ass, the thieving bastard!"***

I let the matter ride for a week making sure not to speak to Locky or make any enquiries about Errol's whereabouts to avoid raising any suspicion. Soon after, I saw Errol in East Ham and I asked him how he was and asked if he wanted to come around to play cards. He said sure, so we agreed that he would come around that evening.

That night he arrived around 8am and I decided to lay a little trap just to see whether my suspicions were accurate or not. I needed to test this little thieving bastard to satisfy myself that I wasn't mistaken. So I came up with a little plan there and then. At that time, I smoked around 20 cigarettes per day so I asked Errol if he wanted a coffee before we began our evening of playing cards. He said "yes" so I made my way down to the kitchen making sure to leave the cigarette packet containing 18 in plain view.

Upon returning upstairs while the kettle was boiling, I reached for the packet and, without making it too obvious, I counted the cigarettes in the packet**. "Gotcha!"** I thought to myself- sure enough there were 4 or five missing: this guy was clearly an opportunist and a petty thief.

First I returned to the kitchen and made his cup of coffee, all the while trying to suppress the rage that was building up. I then returned upstairs and presented him with the steaming beverage. Would you believe it, the cheeky bastard actually winced when he tasted it, saying it was **"a bit strong!**" Can you believe this, I thought? Not only was he pilfering cigarettes from under my nose, but he had the temerity to complain about the coffee after stealing my birthday present!

Without warning, I rushed at him. All of the anger which had built up after my tape recorder went missing came to the surface and I went to town on him, aiming punches at his head, pinning him to the carpet and pummelling away at him while he croaked and snivelled, pleading for me to stop. I eventually stopped only when I became tired, at which point I grabbed him by his jumper and dragged him down the few steps to the lower level and threw him down to the bottom of the stairs where he lay, only slightly moving. Following him down, I opened the front door of the house and hauled him out of the hallway and dumped him on the path outside. After a couple of minutes of watching him lying there, he eventually hauled himself to his feet, all the while groaning with one hand clutching his back, before shuffling away up on the path and out of sight with a hop and drop movement.

I half expected the police to come to the property, as I was sure someone must have heard the commotion, but no one came.

"Good, I thought – that'll teach the little scumbag to steal my property!"

I didn't encounter Errol again until about a month later when there was an almighty crash from downstairs one evening and I rushed downstairs to find that a brick had been hurled at the front door shattering the glass.

I ran out to see someone, whom I believe to be Errol, riding away into the distance at pace on a bicycle. Had I been closer I would have ran after him and kicked him off the bike. I never saw him again.

The landlord wasn't too happy at having to stump up the cash for the repairs but didn't make too much of a fuss and It would be many months before I told my mother about the stolen tape recorder and subsequent events.

Like the events at Goodmayes, the cumulative sequence of events and sheer excessiveness of drink, late nights and partying at Margery Park Road meant that things were bound to come to a sudden and shuddering halt. This happened for two reasons :

One: One Saturday, in the middle of a party at Malcolm and Tony's place, they got a tip-off that the house was going to be raided so everyone got busy flushing away pills, hash and other paraphernalia. Seldom had I seen people spring into action so quickly. Not long after that, the front door splintered and in rushed, not the police but Lemmon, a rival dealer and his cronies. They held us up with guns and baseball bats while they searched the house for the stash of "gear" and money but found nothing but some loose cash in drawers. They departed almost as suddenly as they had appeared warning us to stay put. I escaped with a sore sternum after being jabbed very hard with the end of a baseball bat but learned months later that I had got off pretty lightly. Apparently Lemmon told someone that had we retaliated, I would have got it first because I looked most likely to be troublesome due to my short hair which contrasted sharply to the other guys long hippy locks.

Two: After this visit from Lemmon, Malcolm and Tony felt that it would have drawn too much attention from the landlord who had to fork out for another repair job, the police and other rivals in the area so it was decided that they would carry out a sting which consisted of selling a large amount of fake hashish. If the sale went okay, all well and good. If not, there would have to be a violent conclusion. Suffice to say that the transaction downstairs did not go well. The chosen day was a Sunday and we had been advised to make ourselves scarce and not visit the downstairs apartment. I had a couple of friends around that evening and we heard the sound of people arriving downstairs so we kept as quiet as field mice.

After what seemed like an eternity, but which was actually a few minutes of muffled conversation between the two groups of transactors below, there was a sudden escalation of activity, shouts of accusation, angry threats followed by one hell of a commotion culminating in screams of pain. Then silence. After a couple of minutes, we heard the sound of the front door closing, followed by the departure of cars.

We found out later from the police that the would be buyers had been severely beaten with baseball bats and left in pools of blood, their buttocks slashed with razors and their money was taken. That was the last we heard or saw of Malcolm and Tony. Further information was relayed to us by the paramedics who eventually attended at the scene. They explained that gang members often slash rivals across the arse, as there is less chance of them leaping into a vehicle to pursue you. Several weeks later we heard from a source that Tony and Malcolm had fled to

Scotland but this was never confirmed as we never saw or heard of them again.

Within a matter of days, the landlord had got wind of the recent events at the property, decided that enough was enough and gave notice to vacate which I did and hastily made plans to move on yet again. Given the recent violent events at the address, and the premises almost becoming a hippy commune, I was actually very happy to be moving on.

CHAPTER SEVENTEEN

Back to Bedlam:

"Home is where you go when you run out of places".

As a stop gap, I arranged to move in temporarily with Dad, who had since moved from Hackney to a flat in Philip Lane, Tottenham. Although he was initially very welcoming it soon became very obvious that all was not well with his state of mind.

Over the next couple of weeks after many conversations with the young couple who lived beneath him, I learned that he slept very little at night and could be heard walking around until the early hours. This became evident to me also after noticing that long after turning in for the night, the light remained on in the hallway outside my room and he would approach quietly and then stand silently for ages outside the door.

Apart from the discomfort of being in a room with no heating, the window panes all had holes in the glass which let in the frost and cold winds. Dad not only refused to turn the heating on but simply couldn't be bothered to have the broken panes of glass replaced by the association that managed the property. I found his behaviour and the conditions extremely unsettling so I actually wasn't planning on being there for too long, but equally, I wasn't prepared for a sudden turn of events.

On around the fourth week of being there, I came home from work and upon reaching the top of the stairs I called out a cheery **"Hi Dad, I'm home!"** upon which he hastily darted out of his bedroom, ran into the lounge and quickly locked the door. Within a matter of minutes, the front doorbell sounded so I went downstairs and opened it, only to find two policemen standing outside.

"**Are you Mr Bellamy?"** one of them asked, looking at me suspiciously. I replied that I was. He asked me to step outside onto the area leading into the property. It was then explained to me that Dad had called them during the day and told them I was being very disruptive and that he wanted me to leave. He had clearly given them a rough idea of what time I arrived home each day. I began to relate a brief history of dad's behaviour and mental health issues but, in short, they said as it was his home, he had the right to have me removed, so while they stood outside the premises, I went upstairs and removed item by item, everything I had moved in a few weeks prior. During this activity, Dad remained camped in the lounge avoiding any conversation or contact of any kind with me. It was only when everything belonging to me had been removed from the premises, that the officers asked for my house key, which I gave them. They then departed, leaving me standing there with all my personal belongings, clothes, small bits of furniture, records etc. piled up in the front garden near the sidewalk. It was really embarrassing and to say I was angry would be an understatement.

From the pavement, every now then whenever I glanced up at the window above, the curtains would move slightly so I knew Dad was watching me all the time. I walked down the road to a public phone box and called a couple of guys I knew in Stoke Newington.

"What – your father dashed you out of the house, just like that? Just like that?" was the question, over and over again.

Eventually, they got the picture after I shouted: ***"Yes – Just like that for fuck sake, now are you going to help me or not?".*** They drove over and helped me load my belongings into a small van and between the two of them they agreed to store the larger items until I had sorted out somewhere to move to. I then phoned Mum, who was now living in Highbury and having explained Dad's erratic behaviour, it was decided that I would stay in a spare room at her place until I found a new place. Within a week I had found digs in Defoe Road, Stoke Newington with Mum's help so again I was on the move once more and ironically, very near to familiar places like Stamford Hill, Mare Street, Ridley Road and Downs Park. Suddenly, it was almost like coming home.

CHAPTER EIGHTEEN

The Wrong Number

Looking back at the years after my years away from North London, the ensuing period would prove to be life-changing and full of incidents best described as "character building".

It was during this time that I met Trevor Murrell, like me an aspiring musician and a fellow Barbadian. Trevor was a very good drummer and played in a band in The Three Crowns on Church Street, Stoke Newington at the weekend. Sometimes he would invite me up on stage to play along with them.

Trevor always carried a pair of drumsticks and I recall the many times he came around to my flat and after placing two kitchen chairs in front of him, he would get his sticks out and knock the merry hell out of them. The chairs eventually ended up with the stuffing hanging out of the seat.

Whilst playing for a local band, I was approached by another set of musicians, the Aces, who used the same rehearsal studio on alternate nights. The timing of this event couldn't have come at a better time as I was getting tired of playing at black-tie dinner and dance gigs.

During this period I began dating a girl who I had met in rather unusual circumstances. I was working part-time in a store and one day, the in branch telephone rang so, noticing that no one else was rushing to take the call, I answered it. The female on the other end of the line enquired about someone and I replied that she must have the wrong number. That should have been the end of it. I'm not even sure how, but suffice to say that, being a bit green around the gills I began chatting away with the young woman and before I knew it, she had invited me out for a date and I accepted. And so the dating game commenced and within a few months, we were discussing finding a place to live.

The readers will recall that I had grown up in a household where domestic arguments were commonplace and my father, riven by self-doubt, paranoia and insecurity, never hesitated in handing out a thrashing to my mother or myself. It's a sad indictment on society that historically, unlike today, the law seemed to turn a blind eye to domestic violence and men such as him commonly referred to as "beaters", revelled in this lack of lawful oversight or intervention.

Shamefully, in the UK, it wasn't even until 1875, that a law was passed, which then made it illegal for a woman to be beaten between the hours of 10pm and 7am, purely on the grounds that the commotion might disturb the neighbours, thereby proving that the law can indeed be an ass.

It wasn't too long after moving in together that I found out to my cost that she had, what is best described as, severe anger management issues which manifested itself in her launching herself into a violent rage at the slightest cause or dissent, and at anything spoken, inferred or regarded as provocation. During one of these attacks after I had entered the room where she was standing with her back to me, she whirled around and struck me flush on thc bridge of my nose with an unopened can of cola without warning. My head exploded with pain as my nose was opened to the bone and blood sprayed from the wound. She looked at my bloodied face and rushed from the room screaming. Off to the hospital I went, nose patched up, reassurances offered by my attacker and her family that it wouldn't happen again, I returned home.

It wasn't too long before there was another incident.

On that occasion after I arrived home from a gig a little later than planned, she flew at me with a kitchen knife, shouting: ***"One of your sluts phoned here for you!"*** Even though I managed to flee to a room and lock the door, she actually hacked through the wooden panel, unlocked the door and rush at me with a large glass ashtray. How I managed to avoid a crushing blow to the face I'm not sure, but avoided it I did and exited the room at some pace and retreated to the security of the street for my own safety. Well, I'm not sure who the imaginary slut was, because I certainly didn't know any. For one thing, I would never have been that stupid, to hand out my home telephone number to another female with such a wild and unpredictable woman at home.

I wandered the nearby streets for an interminable period before cautiously returning home to find my previously frenzied attacker now calm, apologetic and apparently full of remorse.

It later turned out that one of my fellow band members had given it out "for a bit of fun" as he termed it. Little did he know that his idea of fun nearly got me seriously injured or worse.

After the third or fourth attack, this time after she clearly objected to my reply to a comment she made, she rushed at me with a hot iron which was still plugged in the socket and wire sparking wildly as it was ripped from the wall. I only avoided having my face burned and disfigured by sidestepping her lunge and pushing her to one side before making a hasty escape out of the room and into the street yet again and staying there until she had calmed down. This was the pattern, like a recurring bad dream.

Despite the reassurances from her parents that they would make sure she got some treatment for these dangerous outbursts, I was nearing my limit. The truth was, one never knew when the next attack would come.

One morning, in the sanctity of my locked room, I woke up and thought: *"I really must bring this to an end. This is no way to live. What If I retaliate to defend myself and she ends up seriously injured?"* How many times had men after being attacked by a partner, called the police, and ended up being escorted out of the premises as the aggressor?

It was probably that fear, as much as the fear for my own safety, which finally gave me the impetus to take some form of action.

I'd had enough. I knew then that if I stayed, someone would get very badly hurt or worse. So one morning, I got up early, got dressed and left, taking only the clothes on my back and leaving all else behind. And I didn't return despite the impeachments and promises from the wild banshee of a woman. Personally, I think she could have given Mike

Tyson a run for his money, she was that belligerent and aggressive.

Did I see her again after that? In ensuing months, she would occasionally turn up at a venue or at wherever I was staying, having somehow found out the address and attempt to convince me to return, but it was out of the question.

The saying "Misery acquaints a man with strange bedfellows" was never truer when I reflect on that turbulent but thankfully short relationship.

And so, onto the music.

Desmond Dekker was one of many highly successful Jamaican singers who gained fame during the seventies back in Jamaica. His hits included The Israelites, Pickney Gal and You can get it if you really try. It was extremely expensive flying an entire band to and fro when it came to touring so like many other artists, he took the practical option of using London based session musicians for British tours.

Besides Dekker, we worked frequently for Brother Roy Shirley (FEEL GOOD) and Tito Simon (THAT MONDAY MORNING

FEELING), both of whom had also recorded many hits both in Jamaica and in England. Between them, we were kept very busy around all parts of Britain playing at clubs up north and the midlands and larger gigs in London. Eventually, all of these singers relocated permanently to British shores.

The highlight of the year was always when major artists like Dennis Brown, Barrington Levy and Ken Booth toured the UK. We knew we'd be very busy indeed and looked forward to the huge gigs at The Lyceum and the Empire Leicester Square.

The Aces (with a now reinvented Herol Burton on backing vocals, still a bit of a dandy but now presenting himself as a Rastaman, complete with little dreadlocks and shouting out "Jah Rastafari" and constantly quoting phrases from The Book of The Maccabees at every opportunity) were just one of many such in demand bands supporting these internationally acclaimed artists: The Cimarrons, The Undivided, Black Slate and Jamaican Express were, like us, some of the hardest working around and there existed amongst us a friendly but competitive rivalry.

If you were a musician living in London at that time, it was virtually impossible to avoid bumping guitar cases with another player as you turned a corner. It was customary for many of us all to meet up backstage before a big show and discuss who we were working with.

In spite of the camaraderie that existed, we all kept a very professional eye on each other, keeping tabs on what equipment the other was using: drummers regarded each other with steely attention, while guitar players watched each other keenly seeing if they could pick up on or even copy any fancy licks displayed by a rival from the secrecy of the curtains at side-stage.

On one occasion Bob Marley, who was in London on his own tour walked into the dressing room area and wished the band members good luck for the show. To be honest, we were all rather star-struck to be in the same space as this diminutive man with a strong presence.

In our dressing rooms, food, a lot of alcohol, tobacco and other substances best described as "vegetable matter", were always available, and its no exaggeration to say that my bandmates revelled in the excess. I once read an article in an American music magazine which stated that many guys "only want to be in a band to get chicks" and on the evidence of some of the antics witnessed on the road, I have to say that's probably damn true. After each performance, there was always females hammering on the dressing room door for autographs, and phone numbers, so it's fair to say that some of the guys took full advantage of this fan worship with a lot of frantic groping and exchanging of body fluids taking place in adjoining dressing rooms.

During this period, I kept in regular contact with my father who had by now spent a couple of spells under section in Claybury psychiatric hospital, but he always discharged himself after a short period. I remember on one particular occasion going to visit him at his Philip Lane flat and invited him over to my place to have dinner with me and my partner.

All was going well until about an hour after we had eaten. I was clearing the table when I heard a shuffling behind me and

I began to turn to see what it was. Before I could spin around fully, Dad was upon me and had struck me over my head with a bottle which, although it shattered, only stunned me. I fell to my knees clutching my head and felt blood trickling through my fingers. Luckily, it wasn't as serious an injury as it felt at the time. Before we could fully comprehend what had happened, Dad had rushed through the door of the flat, down the stairs and out onto the street. From the window I could see him running to the bus stop whereupon he leapt onto a bus heading back to Tottenham. Yes, Dad was very unpredictable. It would be many months before I actually got to speak with him at length. Whenever I visited him, If he spoke to me at all, it would be from a window saying "The spirits told him" he shouldn't let me in. It would be several months more before I managed to persuade dad to allow me through the front door and into his abode and even then he would watch me suspiciously for several minutes before engaging in tentative conversation.

As for my musical adventures, like all things, everything comes to an end or changes direction, and after four years of crazy touring around and being away from home for many weekends I decided to leave the Aces band. Some of the members had become very complacent and acted like they were Gods gift to music and even refused to rehearse at times and would spend much studio time sitting at a table playing dominoes. In addition, a few of us were tiring of playing Dekker's Rock Steady and Ska type of reggae which incidentally should be given huge credit for laying the foundations for the British Two Tone Movement which came later and acts such as The Specials, Madness, The Beat and Bad Manners achieving huge success. To be honest, I much preferred to be in the studio working on tracks instead of being on stage. Put it down to my natural shyness I guess which meant I always felt slightly uncomfortable with so many eyes focused in me. Ironic as it may sound, the music we played often attracted large numbers of skinheads and it was these who attended some of our gigs and bopped around and wildly applauded each number, that might well have been amongst any bunch of rogue "skins" that cornered you in an alleyway the following night and gave you a damn good kicking for being black and in the wrong place at the wrong time. Listen to Linton Kwesi Johnson's "Story of Jim" and you'll get an idea of the fate that could befall a lone black male confronted by Skins in an alley.

Two or three of us, thoroughly disillusioned, were keen to try our hands at something different, even commercial pop music. The style of music we were playing then was clearly appreciated by aficionados of softer reggae and predominantly white audiences but not very well received by those who preferred a more "rootsy" style. As a result, especially when playing at the black clubs notorious for giving artists little, or no respect if you tested their patience, certain members of the band would carelessly hit wrong notes or begin a song in the wrong key, which would often result in one of the sound system crew simply unplugging the electricity. Clubs like The Santa Rosa in Birmingham, the Bouncing Ball in Peckham or The Bronx Club in Stoke Newington were well known for drowning a band out with their sound system If they didn't like what they were hearing. Playing at such venues, you very quickly learned that if they didn't boo you, you must be doing okay. These tough audiences seldom applauded, they simply nodded stoically in time to the music and permitted you to finish your set and remain on the stage without heckling and then turning off the power. If they *really hated* what you were playing, it would only be a matter of minutes before someone would give full vent to their annoyance and declare, making good use of Jamaican expletives: ***"But what the bloodclaat – Hey, MC –switch off dat raas and turn back on de sound!"*** Within seconds the ear-shattering **BOOF BOOF** of the sound system which start up with deafening output, the crowd would turn away and get back to their skanking, and we would unplug instruments, dismantle everything and get the hell out, slinking away like whipped curs.

Roy Shirley was the only singer of the three we worked with that seemed to have the respect of these tough crowds. Here was a singer who didn't just walk onto the stage and belt out his hits. Here was a man who loved to put on a bit of a show for his audience. I recall the first time we worked with him. As the MC, then Duke Alloy but later known as Astro from UB40, announced his name and we started the intro to the first number, we expected him to emerge from stage right as Dekker used to do, but instead we were baffled to see the packed audience slowly parting from the back of the auditorium. As the throng at the front parted, we were amazed to see Roy emerge from the cheering crowd flanked by two men in white coats and, him wearing a straight jacket. As he mounted the stage, the 'attendants' would remove his restraint for him to begin his set. I must say he played the mad man extremely well, much to the delight of his audience. Brother Roy, as he was affectionately referred to by his fans, passed away some years ago but leaves behind a strong musical legacy.

CHAPTER NINETEEN

Coconuts

Dictionary definition: *"The coconut tree is a member of the family Areaceae and the only species of the genus Cocos, the fruit of which is a large hairy brown nut which is found throughout the world's tropical islands and countries."*

Alternative definition: An offensive term which is used to accuse someone of betraying their race or culture by implying that, like a coconut, they are brown on the outside but white on the inside. Another racial term used to imply that a black person is "acting white" is called a "Bounty Bar" or Oreo. The assumption seems to be that if as a black person one consorts with dates, marries or socializes with a white person, they have rejected their own heritage and somehow retreated into a world of whiteness and modern day neo-colonial subjugation. Where a black man is observed to speak with anything akin to a refined accent, one can vehemently be accused of "talking like a white man!". I read a magazine article in which a young black woman wrote with some venom that she absolutely "hates black men that date or marry outside of their race". The vitriol with which the piece was written made it abundantly clear that if she had her way, she would welcome the immediate reintroduction of the death penalty for these offenders. It was obvious that the bitter aftertaste of slavery and past colonialism still lingers within the very core section of the afro- Caribbean community and many would say with good rcason. Whilst there are many who might readily share her view, there are those who, without forgetting or denying our past history, find it more practical to focus on modern day instances of racial prejudice and inequality.

Whilst blacks that have white friends are, rather unimaginatively referred to as "coconuts" or even "Choc -Ices", I learned with some amusement that where the reverse is observed, namely whites having black friends or partners, they are sometimes referred to as "mince pies", a comparison to that popular Christmas confection which is light in colour on the outside but dark inside".

How many people remember the ground-breaking Sydney Poitier film, "Guess who's Coming to Dinner?" in which a middle-class white girl had the temerity or courage, depending on how the individual sees it, to bring home a black man to meet her parents and the furore which ensued.

During the 1980's I hung out and partied with a group of black lads around North

London. I was intrigued somewhat to observe that not one of them had a black girlfriend or partner, every female was white British.

On the flip side of that, I can also say that I have known several English guys whom I have never on any occasion seen with a white partner. Geoff, Mick, Chris and Bing always dated black girls from a West Indian or African background and probably consumed more typically Caribbean food than their black friends. Apart from his obvious penchant for Afro-Caribbean women, Bing was best known for having been the butt of a particularly cringe-worthy prank at one of Mick's parties. His surname was Crosbie, so like many other people with that surname he inevitably ended up being given the tag of Bing after the American crooner.

It was customary at Mick's parties for all of the contents of half-empty bottles to be emptied into a large container and then brought into the kitchen after which, upon hearing the cry "Moonshine!!" everyone would take a plastic cup, plunge it into the murky liquid comprised of beer, whisky, vodka and several other spirits, and tip it down one's neck to loud cheers. Well, if you weren't already drunk, it wouldn't be too long before it took effect and one would be throwing one's legs all around to the music like a deranged contortionist. Bing was one of them. Within half an hour he was so inebriated that he had passed out and had to be carried upstairs to sleep it off. We all forgot about him as the party got into full swing and it wasn't until several hours later around 3am, that we noticed the unfortunate Bing re-emerge, supported by two other party-goers, but this time completely naked. After making their way through the gyrating party-goers, he was laid out on a sofa fully uncovered, and much to the amusement of the revellers, left in the full glare of us all to snore away in his alcoholic stupor. You can imagine his surprise when he eventually stirred several hours later and found himself completely naked in the middle of a frantic party, upon which he looked around in absolute horror, leapt to his feet, covered his exposed genitals and sprinted upstairs covering himself as best as he could. I'm not sure why he bothered trying to conceal his privates, after all, they have been on show for several hours anyway, and considering the speed with which he dashed upstairs, perhaps we should have renamed him 'Bolt'.

Whenever you bumped into Mick or Geoff, they both spoke in an affected West Indian patois and would throw in the occasional Jamaican expletive such as ***"Bumba Claat",*** just to demonstrate that they we're "down with the brothers" and could speak some patois. As you can imagine this initially raised quite a few eyebrows. What made this even more bizarre was the fact that most of the West Indian lads spoke with typically regional Cockney accents, prompting someone to observe plaintively on one occasion that *"black guys don't even talk like black guys anymore!"* This comment being a clear reference to the sad parody of West Indian accents offered by controversial comedians of the day such as Jim Davidson and Bernard Manning both of whose vile racial impersonations on TV and on stage became their stock and trade and made them household names.

More than once, a member of the assembled group of lads would get a bit irritated and ask Mick or Geoff: **"Why are you talking like that for?"** This only prompted him to risk a punch in the mouth by responding with an even more exasperating reply such as: **"Easy nuh, or Cool Nuh man?".** Chris even walked with an exaggerated swagger. The truth is that these young men had all grown up with and around black males, had picked up the lingo and had stuck with it. Were they trying to "act black?" or just trying to be "cool?" In choosing black females as partners and adopting this West Indian style of speaking, was it through choice?, Had they somehow betrayed their race and rejected their own culture?. Perhaps they were, like their black counterparts, simply exercising their right to date or live with whoever they wanted to. For making those choices you can be sure that these white guys occasionally had to endure a great deal of offensive attention from sections of the white community who would, for example, shouted out derisive, but sadly unimaginative comments such **as "What's the matter – couldn't you find a white woman then!"**- at least this is what Geoff told us.

On a return trip from Barbados, I was queuing at a food counter behind an interracial couple when I observed the girl serving behind the counterpoint at the tray of chicken and ask the black guy with a mischievous glint in her eye: **"Do you prefer white meat or dark meat Sir?"** Now I'm pretty damn sure that some guys faced with this kind of barefaced impudence may well have struck back with a reply like: **"And what's it to you, bitch?"** It wasn't evident whether he was even taken aback or not but to his credit he calmly replied: **"I don't care what colour the meat is, so long as it tastes good!"** and gave her a cheeky wink.

I guess the woman serving behind that counter must have come into contact with many such couples on a weekly basis and I wonder if she gave them all a hard time just for the sheer hell of it. Is this an example of racism, or was it simply a personal bias? Well, there is a saying which goes: ***"If it walks like a duck, and quacks like a duck, then, it's a duck!"***.

From that incident alone, it became starkly clear that, even in this, the 21st

Century, there are still many islanders who are quick to apply the "coconut" tag and appear to regard the very presence or sight of an interracial couple or children of mixed heritage, as unpalatable, unwelcome or totally abhorrent.

It's not for me to say whether they are right or not to have this attitude, and none of us should ever forget or disregard the stain on history that slavery has left, however, there are many who, whilst not forgetting the past, would prefer to focus their attention on the present and the future.

In fairness, I should add that Barbados, is also the only place that whilst visiting, and upon entering a doctors waiting room, every single person to a man or woman, greeted ones entrance with a hearty "Good morning!" It is truly a place of sharp contrasts where I personally found many of the folks welcoming but also experienced or heard examples of regressive and hostile behaviour. Much like my late mother who upon re-entering Barbados after returning from England where she had attended the funeral of her partner of forty years. She related, with an amount of wry humour, how the customs official had reacted when in response to being asked for evidence of the reason for her hasty return to England. Upon taking out and presenting a photograph of Tony, who happened to be English, lying in his coffin, the official barely able to avoid bursting a blood vessel, looked at her and said with incredulity: ***"A white man, a white man??"*** Mum went on to say that in response she gave have him a mouthful of invectives laced with her customary F's and C's and made her way out the customs hall. The fact is, as a "returnee" to Barbados after spending many years abroad in a foreign country, one is treated with scant regard, as Mum knew. Her experience led me to wonder whether this was the reason why, in the forty years together, she and Tony never actually visited Barbados together. Was she conscious of the possible adverse reaction she would receive?

A young black lad I was working with took great offence one day when I commented that a particular song by the Eagles was a great composition. Seething with anger he asked me: **"Are you a sell-out?"** The truth is, that even as a lad I had a fascination with cowboy books and movies. I could happily sit and watch Gunsmoke, Rawhide or The Virginian for days if allowed. By the age of 16 had I not only read about The James gang, together with the Younger brothers, the Daltons and Buffalo Bill to name a few, and if asked I could probably have told you the type of horse ridden by each cowboy, whether it was a Palomino, a Bay, Roan or Appaloosa. Although I enjoy and play all styles and genres of music, I believe that is where my liking for the music of Eagles founder members Don Henly and Glen Frey stemmed from and as a guitar player myself, the more chords a song has, the more I like it.

In a further attempt to stereotype me, my protagonist had the temerity to suggest, with eyes popping out of his head and through gritted teeth, that as a black person I should only listen to or buy music by black artists. He finished his tirade by telling me that I should be ashamed of myself. I can't deny that I was very tempted to use the "F" word followed by "Off "and tell him where to go but instead decided not to waste my time explaining my musical tastes to him, choosing instead to ignore him. To those who might have the same views as that individual, be reassured that in spite of the number of times I've listened to "Hotel California", "Tequila Sunrise" or "New Kid in Town", I'm definitely still black whenever I look in the mirror the following day.

It was producer Chris Blackwell who convinced Bob Marley that if he wanted to "cross -over "and break into the more commercial markets in Europe and America, that he would have to make his music more attractive to new audiences, so that's where Al Anderson, with his blues/rock style of guitar playing came in, although Marley at first resisted it by remarking: **"I don't like what him a play!"** His producer, albeit with some difficulty, eventually managed to persuade Marley to accept Anderson who went on to become an integral member of the Wailers right up to Marley's untimely death.

I imagine that my former colleague would have spat in indignation to learn that one of America's most revered and successful heavy metal bands is an African American outfit named Living Colour, fronted by guitarist Vernon Reed. What would the music world be without acts like Hooty and the Blowfish led by Darius Rucker, a multi talented black musician from Charleston, USA and let's not forget Lennie Kravitz (born of a white Russian father and an Afro American mother), Roachford and Seal. He would probably regard them all as turncoats and Uncle Toms.

As music lovers, we heap praise on all of those prominent and successful artists such as Bob Marley, Marvin Gaye, Luthor Vandross, Earth Wind and Fire and all of those other wonderfully talented black musicians, but I have always regarded it as a mistake to close our ears to other music styles and deprive ourselves of the myriad of fantastically diverse material there is on offer. After all, oranges are definitely not the only fruit as they say.

Every black boy who ever picked up a guitar and dared to dream of mastering the instrument in a manner which would make people sit up and take notice, owe a huge amount of thanks to artists like Jimi Hendrix for bursting onto the music scene and shaking up a rock world that had previously been dominated by established stalwarts such as Eric Clapton, Jimmy Page and Jeff Beck.

This artistic catharsis was as ground breaking as the so called Blaxploitation films, a sub-genre of the early exploitation films, which suddenly emerged in the early 70's. These films were originally made for black audiences but were so successful that their appeal broadened across racial and ethnic lines. Titles such as Blacula (a Dracula parody), Shaft (Starring Richard Roundtree), Cleopatra Jones, Black Belt Jones, Cool Breeze, saw movie goers of all colours queuing at the ticket offices. I can still recall the death scene played out by Antonio Fargas, as gangster Doodle Bug in Cleopatra Jones, when as he lay shot and dying on the ground, he still found the strength to reach up and pat his huge afro into shape. These really were the days of "The 'fro".

For the first time here was a new and exciting group of actors and characters. This was a refreshing and long overdue departure from the fare served up in the early 1930's by Lincoln Perry who is generally regarded to have been America's first black movie star. He used the film pseudonym of Steppin Fetchett, and his characters often portrayed and personified the stereotypical slave who pretended to be lazy, servile and dim-witted, in order to fool or wrong foot his white masters. After years of seeing blacks portrayed predominantly as servants and field hands, black cinema goers flocked to movies such as Buck and The Preacher starring Harry Belafonte and Sidney Poitier and their success paved the way for the emergence of other male stars latterly by the likes of Woody Strode, Laurence Fisburne, Wesley Snipes, Samuel L Jackson, Denzil Washington, Eddie Murphy and Will Smith. The movie world was further enriched by equally talented female actors, the likes of Pam Greer of Jackie Brown fame, Robin Givens, Angela Bassett, Lela Rochon and Viveca A Fox. It was the 1939 classic film, Gone With the Wind, set against the background of the American Civil War in the deep South, which gave the industry its first black Oscar winner. Hattie Mcdaniel won the Academy Award for her portrayal of the enslaved house servant Mammy.

On British television, programmes such as Love Thy Neighbour, The Lennie Henry Show and above all, The Real McCoy brought a host of characters to our screens which sought to break down racial barriers by taking a comedic look at predominately male gender stereotypes within our communities and making us laugh at ourselves a little. The latter featured performers such as Leo Chester, Robbie Gee and particularly the late and greatly missed, Felix Dexter who gave us classic cameos such as the London Underground ticket collector who spoke like a pigeon, the lascivious African pastor who delivered sermons to his congregation about virtue whilst all the time casting a lecherous eye over the females present and the posh black man doing his utmost to attain some street credibility and appear 'more black' by attempting to speak Jamaican patois in an upper crust English accent. Perhaps we all recognized a little of ourselves, or of someone we knew in these characters. Even I, having developed a pronounced English accent over the years as a result of being raised here, have at times been viewed as, and labelled of being a little *"too English"* by people of my own race who would no doubt struggle to believe that I knew anything at all about my own roots or of black history and culture.

I wonder how many people can empathise with my experience of returning to my place of birth for a holiday after many years of settling and integrating into a foreign culture, only to find themselves in the invidious and unenviable position of being treated as "foreigners" by the local inhabitants. Imagine my surprise and embarrassment after opening my mouth to order a drink in a bar or order a meal in a restaurant, only to be greeted by comments such as: ***"Ahaaa – we have an Englishman here!".*** Or the even more disparaging response from amused locals who upon hearing my accent could only offer: ***"But listen to him – he talkin' like a white man".***

It is no wonder why so many of us immigrants from the Islands struggle to understand where we actually fit in and crave for the ever elusive answer to that burning question: Where do we actually belong? We are in effect, an unhomed people, many of whom bear the weight of displacement on their shoulders.

CHAPTER TWENTY

Midsomer Madness

Midsomer Murders is a popular detective series set in the fictional county of Midsomer which is made up of several picturesque little villages in which there are cosy little pubs, village greens, and where daily life is punctuated by activities such as fetes and fayres. The series has run from 1997 to date.

What makes Midsomer quite original, in the first instance, is the extremely high number of murders which occur here and which as a result keeps the principal character Tom Barnaby and his assistants rather busy. The second anomaly which strikes one immediately upon watching the program is the absence of any black characters whatsoever. Having watched many episodes over the years

I find no shame in admitting that I have never failed to enjoy immensely the story lines which seem to follow a pretty routine format. It is, after all, fiction, and I readily accept that the settings and characters in the shows are pretty representative of typical English village life, so for me, no surprises here at all. Programmes like Midsomer feature settings one would expect to find in parts of Britain such as Devon and Cornwall, where the racial mix is typically 94 to 98 percent white with perhaps a smattering of other races, which includes Asian, those of mixed race, and some of the various European origins. Statistics show that a black person in Devon, whose number is, as of writing, approximately 400, is nine times more likely to be stopped than their white counterpart. One famous actress who spent much of her childhood in Cornwall, and whose father is white and her mother a black Zambian, recounts how miserable her childhood was due to her family being racially abused as they walked through the town centre. She describes the people in this part of England as "rather backward". She stopped short of labelling this behaviour as racist.

Other visitors to the region noted that it felt rather like "going back in time" and its fair comment to mention that even a white colleague at my office said after visiting that even he felt somewhat uncomfortable at times and that he found the locals rather "cliquish". Upon hearing this, and despite my own challenges growing up, I was immediately reminded of how wonderfully diverse London is and how accepting the majority of its citizens are.

On another occasion, a black co-worker of mine, after returning from a weekend in Cornwall, told me of the reception he received upon entering a village pub. While he was standing at the bar waiting to order drinks for him and his black companion, he overheard a local patron remark loudly: ***"Oh dear – it's got a bit dark in here ain't it?"*** This drew muffled guffaws and chuckles from many of the assembled regulars.

It simply demonstrates how the attitudes of locals can be interpreted and burned into the memory by, lets say English tourists visiting Wales for example. It only takes one person to have a negative experience during their holiday for the word to spread like wildfire.

Contrast these experiences sharply with that of the many white British ex-pats who have made their home in places such as Anguilla, a British overseas territory in the Eastern Caribbean which overlooks neighbouring Saint Martin Island. The ethnic make up here is recorded as 85.3 percent Black/ African, 11.5 per cent Hispanic / Asian and only 3.2 per cent white.

Known for its several offshore islets, long stretches of sandy beaches and secluded coves, Anguilla is described in brochures *as "a warm, welcoming island that captivates its visitors and creates lasting friendships that last a lifetime."*

Indeed, on a TV program which featured Brits who have now happily settled there, one, during an interview ecstatically remarked: *"The people here are so friendly, it's just like being in Cornwall!"*.

It is because of disparities such as this that it is abundantly clear that there still exists a huge societal and cultural imbalance together with a huge chasm in attitudes which may never be bridged.

It would be very easy to immediately brand the ingrained views of those residents of the rural parts of Britain as racist or discriminatory but I willingly concede that their outlook may be partly due to the fact that they have never had to embrace multiculturalism or mass integration and to expect them to do so readily might be akin to asking turkeys to vote for Christmas. When governments, who have long had a love affair with cheap labour encourage mass immigration in order to solve their labour shortages, it's less likely to be for jobs in the outlying rural areas of the country but in the big cities, so the ethnic make up of places such as Cornwall or the so called border counties, for example, would in effect remain pretty much ethnically undiluted, the exception only being where farms, in particular, rely heavily on the labour of workers from Eastern and Central Europe.

The unpalatable truth for "Little Englanders" and "Nimbys"* is that regardless of whether successive governments ever

* Refers to people who are said to have a Not In My Back Yard mentality

succeed in meeting their immigration control targets or not, the fact remains that there is always going to be a need for vegetables to be plucked from the ground, fruit to be picked from trees, coffee to be served in Costa and Starbucks, rooms to be prepared for guests in hotels and personal care tasks to be delivered to the frail and elderly, and the people who invariably fill these jobs hail from that part of the world.

Speaking from experience, having worked in the social care profession for many years, it is clear that this is a field of work which does not attract a large number of the indigenous white population.

In a workforce of 40 carers and support workers, only three were white and it wasn't unusual for the odd one or two new recruits who "gave it a go", to hand in their badges after a day or two, some remarking that "washing arses for a living" wasn't for them, when they found that some of the duties required them to change soiled inco pads, and wash and dress the frail and elderly. I can only assume that they thought all they had to do was to prepare a light meal and then sit and chat for an hour or two. The reason for this? Well, admittedly, the pay is shamefully low, the work often challenging, the hours are unsocial, and the truth is that many folks simply see it as menial work which is too far beneath them. And that, in a nutshell, is why this particular social care sector was then and still is, made up predominantly of workers from the Caribbean, the African continent, South East Asia and now largely supplemented by a contingent of people from Eastern and Central Europe. It is no exaggeration to say that but for those hard-working souls, the members of our ever growing elderly population both in the community and in our care homes, might not have anyone to deliver their most basic of care services.

Many of those born and bred in the rural areas are at least honest enough to state that what others may label as a racist attitude is nothing more than a natural "regional bias" in wanting things to remain preserved as it is.

When a former Prime Minister vehemently protested about the levels of free movement of people from all parts of Eastern Europe, describing the numbers as "hordes", he was likening it some ways to be being invaded by huge unwanted groups. Well, let us put things into true perspective. When the Dutch, Spanish, Belgians, Italians, Germans, French and yes, the English forced their way into the Caribbean, African and other lands over many centuries empire building, *these* were true examples of being invaded. I say, welcome to my world at last.

Can any of us truly say that we are completely free of having had even a degree of subconscious bias towards any individual or group of people?

The hard truth is that all or many of us have a propensity to be racially biased although generally it is never triggered. It is ingrained in the psyche of everyone to some measure, and its origin is rooted in an inherent fear or suspicion of anything or anyone perceived to be vastly different from what we consider to be the norm.

It came as quite a surprise to learn some years ago that the creator of the Midsomer series had been carpeted and severely criticised for remarking that the fictional setting was widely regarded as "The last bastion of Englishness".

The comment caused such an uproar amongst those who, apparently not only found it to be politically incorrect and racist, but also amongst others who had noted the absence of black characters in the series and, clamoured for more diversity in casting. As a result of this reaction, the creator was clearly coerced into making changes when the new series was commissioned.

Now, surprise, surprise, Midsomer now features with what is regarded by many as "token" black and Asian characters in every episode. As well as often featuring one or two central non-white characters, the program throws up the occasional subliminal black actor flitting around in the background, sometimes seen only from the back or as they walk down a corridor and into a room. It has become so predictable that whilst watching an episode recently, I said jokingly: **"Want to wager that an oriental character will appear at some point?"** We weren't disappointed. Within a minute a film extra of East Asian appearance walked into shot, entered a shop and promptly disappeared from view never to reappear as if mysteriously swallowed up by some cinematic black hole.

It would be equally unrepresentative if, for example, a television channel decided to commission a modern day series of Desmond's, that hugely successful series of the 80's which was set in a black barbers shop, but now with a host of white characters. It simply wouldn't mirror or represent the type of establishment or clientele which one can find any day in places such as West Green Road Tottenham, Clapham High Street or Dalston Junction. It would be totally false and misleading. Those of us who are familiar with these areas will probably be aware that within these communities there often exists a somewhat uneasy rivalry, where some West Indians who may be less aware of their ancestry, often refer to Africans as "Boo Boos Men" and the Africans, in turn, call their West Indian counterparts "Those damn Caribbeans".

Midsomer is fiction after all, so this false representation of a typical English village life proves that sometimes it just isn't possible for art to imitate reality. On the plus side, it could be said, that despite this tokenism, the black and Asian actors now featured are probably very grateful for these new work opportunities as it at least gives them the exposure they deserve. My view, however, is that some things simply shouldn't be tampered with simply for the sake of political correctness. Every now and then there is talk of a black James Bond and who would be good for the part. I'm sure there are many excellent black actors who could do a great job, but, no. Let's leave 007 as he is. To do otherwise would just be another case of artistic tokenism.

CHAPTER TWENTY ONE

A Somewhat Moorish Practice

It was once reported that members of the black and Asian community in Birmingham were given reason to complain to the local council when a group of Morris Dancers put on an impromptu display of their talents in Dudley town Centre. It wasn't the dancing that caused offence. It was that this group of performers had the temerity in this day and age to totally "black up" their faces for the performance. Even more appalling was when another troupe managed to get our previously mentioned former Prime Minister to pose with them for a photo at a local festival, although I hasten to add that he wore no black face paint. I wonder whether he would have humoured them so obligingly had he still been in office. Author and broadcaster Bonnie Greer, upon hearing of this, simply called him "a jerk".

These performers, whom some have described as more akin to prancing popinjays than dancers, are most likely to be found scattered around many parts of England, mainly rural areas, outlying country villages and appear typically at fetes and other local events where one might expect to encounter the celebrants doing what country folk do. Being common entertainment in these outlying parts of England, some even practice a form of this dancing known as "Border Morris" which commonly involves blacking up for the event reminiscent of the much-loathed but not lamented Black and White Minstrels of yonder years.

On further investigation, it transpires that when asked the reason for the blacked-up faces, the leader of one of these cohorts offered the rather weak explanation that the custom originated in Medieval times when villagers blackened their faces to hide their identity from any priest who might otherwise recognise and admonish them as pagans.

A plausible explanation perhaps. Upon further investigation, I found documented evidence that although this style of dancing can be traced as far back as the 15th Century, it is suggested that the word Morris is actually derived from the term "Moorish" which refers to a Negro or Arab person. In Shakespeare's Othello the lead character is, after all, a Moor. Ancient figurines of characters appearing to be engaged in a similar style of dancing were sometimes described as being of a somewhat "Moorish" appearance. Furthermore, in some English counties, this style of "Black Face" Morris dancing has apparently often been described as "niggering". I assume that the assembled crowds can enjoy this foul parody, wherever it takes place, in utter privacy, safe in the knowledge that no black person will be in the audience to witness their rapturous enjoyment. An every-day tale of country folk no doubt. They should be reminded that there is a huge difference between comedy and parody.

Even in picturesque Padstow in Cornwall, according to anecdote, it is apparently traditional on Boxing Day and New Year's Day for Morris dancers to parade through town blacked up and singing what they often describe as "minstrel" songs. These days of local celebrations are sometimes referred to as "Darkie Day". After a few complaints from a few visitors from more liberally minded parts of the UK, the Padstonians, all the while denying any racial overtones or intent, on occasion begrudgingly renamed the events "Mummering", blaming "outsiders" for making false claims and trying to cause trouble.

I have been assured, however, that not all Morris Dancers wear the black face paint. I am told that some merely cover their faces with a mask. I know how deeply offended I would be If I ever have the misfortune of stumbling across such a display, after all, it took us until 1978 to rid our screens of the vile Black and White Minstrels although we had to wait until 2008 before the abominable Golliwog character, another insulting parody of a black person, was finally removed from the jars of Robertson's jams.

It must be stated as a counterbalance that there are exceptions in every case and to amplify this, let's take as an example the experience of Wilfred Emmanuel Jones, otherwise known as The Black Farmer.

After arriving from Jamaica in the sixties he settled in Birmingham and carved out a successful career in catering and the media world. However, he had a burning passion for farming and wanted above all to own a piece of land suitable for raising livestock and eventually found such a plot in rural Devon. Despite whatever challenges he encountered, with determination and support from several sources he developed a multi-million-pound business and now has a number of gluten-free products under The Black Farmer brand marketed and available in many outlets in the UK.

A man with a well-known love of flamenco music, Mr Emmanuel proudly states that he is also a lover of Morris dancing and has nothing negative to say about it at all. In fact, he takes part in all of the celebrations with relish and is even more than happy to be photographed doing so. His mantra is "the only cure for fear, is passion", and perhaps, therein lies a lesson for all of us who fear to tread in places where others see only dread and opposition.

A work colleague of mine who comes from Italy, in discussing the issue of race and colour, surprised me by informing me that when growing up as a young boy, he and all of the children he knew, were told by his parents to always fear black people, at least, that is how he interpreted it. He recalled that if they were naughty, their parents would strike dread into them by threatening to call "L'Uomo Nero" (the Black Man) to get them. The imagery of an evil black entity thereby joined the long list of terrifying creatures like The Bogey Man, the Hob Goblin, Rumplestiltskin, The Sack Man, The Headless Nun, The Krampus, an anthropomorphic beast half man, half goat who takes away naughty children, or Spring Heeled Jack. The threat of any of these being summoned was enough to make many of us to cower under the blankets in utter trepidation. I would imagine that every single human being has a fear of something suggested, observed, perceived or imagined:

Creatures of myth, Fiction or fact?
L'uomo Nero, The Man with a Sack,
When The Krampus takes Children, they never come back
The Woman In White, The girl with no face,
The Grim Reaper, those creatures from space,
Rumplestiltskin, his long fingers and feet,
Wide mouthed Clowns with white grinning teeth,
Spectres and Phantoms, dark scary things,
The Jeepers Creepers with huge flapping wings,
The howl of a werewolf, shrill and forlorn,
Zombies and Scarecrows that lurk in the corn,
What do you fear most, what keeps you awake?
What makes you quiver, tremble and shake?
The Thing in the Corner? Fiction or fact?
Shadow Man, Hobgoblin, or Spring Heeled Jack?

In my case, it wasn't any of those. The cause of terror and trepidation was The Woman with no Nose. This was no myth however. There was a middle-aged woman that my mother and I would bump into frequently as we walked down Filey Avenue to the shops.

She had suffered a severe disfigurement to her face leaving her with a large hole where her nose had been. She struck absolute fear into me but, as petrified as I was, I could never tear my eyes away from that black aperture. Mum, being aware of the effect it had on me, would threaten to take me to her house if I misbehaved.

In Holland, there is the Christmas Procession involving a character called "Black Pete", a companion of Saint Nicholas. He is depicted as being of Moorish appearance as he is said to have originated from Spain, again involving blacked up face paint, whilst in Spain itself, there is the curious practice on Epiphany, where family members dress up in costumes to represent characters from the Christmas story but which also often calls for one member of the assembled throng to paint their face black in order to more accurately depict Balthazar, one of the Three Wise Men. It is totally beyond all comprehension why there is such an odd preoccupation with blacking up and the strange obsession with racial mimicry. It came to light recently in the news that even a well known North American

Prime Minister had to face the press and apologise after photographs emerged of him during his college years, with face and arms blacked up attending parties and other functions. In televised statements, he offered that he ***"didn't realize it was racist at the time, but does now!"***

Why should we be surprised at this behaviour or indeed even bother to ask ourselves why some people take pleasure in such despicable entertainment? They do it because as offensive as it may be to black or brown people, they are emboldened to do so because in truth, it's their country, and they regard it as their right to do so *if they so wish.* We, as a people, will constantly be reminded by those who perhaps dream of a land of white only faces, that in the final analysis, the place in which we reside is NOT our country, only the place we call home. To expect behaviour to the contrary would suggest that there exists a parallel universe somewhere, inhabited by flying pigs and pink unicorns.

As the well-known politician Sir Norman Tebbit was quick to point out to the late Darcus Howe, being British through

Naturalization and holding a Passport doesn't make us English any more than an immigrant with a Green card is American. Like it or not, we are in essence, unhomed, displaced people. We should, however, accept that this is where we are, celebrate and uphold all of the traditions attached, and hope that along our journey we are more likely to meet far more supportive and accepting people than those to the contrary.

CHAPTER TWENTY TWO

A Right Royal Conundrum

When it was first reported in the press that Prince Harry was about to announce his intended marriage to American actress Meghan Markle, many of us wondered and speculated what the public reaction would be.

Whilst many people gushed and enthused about the whirlwind romance between the Prince and the celebrity actress, a far more intrusive and darker side began to emerge on parts of the internet.

I recall commenting to a close friend of mine that it wouldn't be too long before mocked up images involving the couple began to appear on the web.

His reply was: "They're on there already!" and promptly sent me a flurry of images via Whatsapp.

It really didn't take much imagination to guess the nature of the images either, many of which I could have predicted. I also feel that depending on how liberal we all are, that some of us may feel some were mildly amusing and others downright offensive and no doubt the newlyweds, who would also have been aware of them, are almost certain to be amongst that number.

Take these examples:

1. Mock up picture of the Queen under a car, with a spanner fiddling with the brakes, dialogue bubble saying: "Marrying a darkie eh, we'll see about that!"
2. Prince Harry, speaking to Prince Phillip, pointing a finger at him and saying: "And don't go trying any of that shit you did with my Mum or my bitch will fuck you up!"
3. Prince Phillip on a tour of Africa, speaking with some natives in grass

skirts and similar head-dress saying to them: "My nephew is marrying one of your lot!"

4. The Queen peering from behind the curtains of a window of Buckingham Palace after the wedding reception asking: "Have the darkies all gone?"

Taking these into account, together with the subsequent preoccupation with constantly stressing how the bride was "of mixed-race heritage" or "the descendant of slaves" in order to add a little spicy controversy to the mix and it becomes evident that whilst many are readily or reluctantly accepting of the Prince's choice, there are clearly those who can already see the foundations of the monarchy creaking and crumbling as they speak.

To them, I say fret not. One young woman of mixed race within the walls of Windsor Castle is in no way going to alter either the historical or social standing of the monarchy, nor significantly affect the lives of ordinary black people in this country.

Furthermore, unbeknown to many, there has been a black bloodline running through the English monarchy for centuries. Recorded in history as The Black Queen, Princess Sophia Charlotte was born in 1752, the eighth child of Charles Louis Frederick, a German Prince and his wife Elisabeth Albertina of Saxe Hildburghausen. As a consequence, Sophia Charlotte was descended directly from an African branch of the Portuguese Royal House of Margarita y Castro Sousa.

She married George 111 of England in 1761 at the age of 17, becoming Queen of England and Ireland after he was chosen to be King due to his lineage as a direct descendant of the Stuart Kings.

The Royal couple had fifteen children, thirteen of whom survived to adulthood. The fourth eldest son, Edward Augustus, the Duke of Kent, later fathered Queen Victoria. Charlotte, therefore, became the great-great-great grandmother of Queen Elizabeth 11.

Queen Charlotte's African bloodline in the Royal family is not common knowledge, having been suppressed for socio-economic reasons. It is believed that popular painters of the day, including Sir Thomas Lawrence who painted her in 1789, were encouraged to "soften" the Queens' "conspicuously Negroid" features, which were evident despite her mulatto or quadroon skin colouring, in order to satisfy the whims of those concerned about the effects of a multi-racial royal family for Britain. It seems that even in today's enlightened times that such a prospect remains a source of extreme irritation for some.

Queen Charlotte died in 1818 at Dutch House in Surrey, now renamed Kew Palace. She is buried at St George's Chapel, Windsor.

CHAPTER TWENTY THREE

The N word- And the Buffalo Connection.

So here we are now in the twenty-first century and we find that black people having settled here have, albeit not without many challenges, integrated quite successfully into most areas of British life and are now somewhat "below the radar". The focus of attention primarily now falls upon a new group of arrivals to the British Isles.

A few months ago I came across a rather disturbing feature on the web which bore the title and asked the question: **"Are Eastern Europeans the New White Niggers?"** The article sought to draw a parallel with the Windrush migration of West Indians to Britain, with the large number of people emigrating from many parts of Eastern Europe in recent years. I hasten to add that while it sought to draw a similarity, it failed and merely succeeded in being offensive to both groups. Our black forbears who travelled here during the Windrush years were invited, as Commonwealth citizens, to emigrate to the Mother country to build up and support the Health Service, Transport systems and many other industries in order to get the economy kick started following the end of the Second World War. The article went on to suggest that modern day migrants, are most likely to be the cause of a noticeable increase in petty and even more serious crime. Popular rhetoric tells us that they are here to take all of the jobs, housing, and wreak irreparable damage on the educational and health services.

Increased migration inevitably calls into question whether many of the new arrivals are in the country legally or illegally and raises suspicions concerning people trafficking, forced labour and modern day slavery. Such a hysterical and divisive political comment is sadly reminiscent of Enoch Powells 1968 "Rivers of Blood" speech which fiercely criticised the level of immigration from Commonwealth countries along with the governments anti-discrimination policies, and does nothing to detoxify the debate about immigration. It seems that whilst black people have managed to assimilate into modern British society with some success, the new arrivals from Eastern and other parts of Europe are, in the main, now reviled, despised and regarded with fear and loathing, much the same as our parents and grandparents were during the Windrush years. A politician was recorded referring to this new group of immigrants as "those people with a 'funny tinge'."

Whilst digesting the subject matter contained in these type of articles, it reminded me of how quick people of limited intelligence seem to enjoy the game of 'pinning a tail on the donkey' by attaching a name to you which relates to your colour in certain situations, for example:

I recall whilst working in retail the odd occasion when a Jewish salesman would refer to their black counterpart as **"the Schwartzer"** (pronounced, *schvaaaartzer*), a derogatory Yiddish term derived from the German language to describe anyone black. I hasten to add that only a few Jewish people I have known over the years have ever openly resorted to such language, the most stark example coming from the mouth of a brash young Jewish salesman I had the misfortune to work with who delighted in describing mental health institutions for Afro Caribbean residents as, **"Homes for crazy Schwartzers!"**

Similarly, a Greek tailor I once worked with constantly referred to me as ***"Mavros"*** (the word for black in Greek) never by my name. It was always: ***"Good morning Mavros!" or "How are you today Mavros?"***

until with steam almost gushing from my head I'd had enough of it and let's just say that I registered my displeasure with such vigour and venom that he never used the term again. I had been forced to act because the more he did it, the more other staff members became emboldened to do the same and ignorantly joined in with impunity. In fact, one particular salesman at the same establishment called me "Mavros" repeatedly, day after day, so relentlessly that finally, in total frustration, I had to take *him* to one side and give him a couple of options which involved me gripping him firmly by the throat and shoving him violently up against a wall. With his eyes bulging and wheezing through his constricted windpipe, he got the message very quickly I can assure you.

I also remember being over at the home of a Turkish neighbour of mine some years ago having coffee and discussing some repair work we were planning to undertake when his cell phone rang. Soon after answering, I was amazed to hear him say in his native language the words, ***"Mavro Arap".*** It was clear that he was telling the caller that he was busy at present speaking with me and that I was black. I cannot for the life of me wonder why he would need to mention my colour or race to the caller. All he needed to say was that he was busy and had a guest. He clearly had no idea that I had a rudimentary understanding of Greek and Turkish, and as consequence, when I challenged him about it, he blustered in embarrassment and offered some garbled, bullshit explanation which served only to make him look or appear even more foolish.

Similarly, the same can be said of the sad habit one particular white South African politician, during the apartheid era, had of referring to black Africans as "kaffirs", often followed by insulting comments such as **"If a kaffir can't eat it, drink it or sleep with it, he doesn't want to know!"** Or, **"You can take a kaffir out of the bush, but you can never take the bush out of a kaffir!"**

In a separate article, I learned that in America, Mexicans are somewhat unceremoniously referred to as "White Niggers" in response to alleged concerns over illegal immigration and crime issues such as drug smuggling. It is worth noting that in both cases, many of these unwanted migrants, both legal and illegal, do much of the menial and low paid jobs which others refuse to do, much to the delight of unscrupulous employers who make a healthy profit by paying shamefully low wages. It is a commonly known fact that as a result of thousands fleeing from modern day conflicts in war torn parts of Africa, the slave block has been given new life with desperate migrants being auctioned off and sold to farmers eager for cheap workers in several European countries.

From time to time, even in these enlightened days, the "N" word, which is described in the dictionary as meaning, "A black or dark-skinned person", still slips from the mouth of those who really should know better. Only this week, a prominent politician, in a closed meeting with others parliamentarians, while discussing the manner in which Britain should leave the European Union resorted to using this epithet. I am sure that she could have employed any other type of rhetoric to make her point, for example, “the devil will be in detail”, “the proof of the pudding” or even, “the fly in the ointment”, but she chose to brazenly declare: **“The real Nigger in the woodpile, will be whether we get a good deal or no deal!”.** This offensive term was first used in the mid to late 18th Century in the deep South of America and referred to slaves who, seeking to escape to the North where slavery was outlawed, used to either conceal themselves in consignments of timber being transported or having escaped, would hide themselves in piles of chopped logs outside people’s houses. To date, the only punishment handed out for this offensive comment was for the Member of Parliament in question to, somewhat reluctantly, offer a rather grudging apology, saying **“it slipped out”,** together with the loss of some parliamentary privileges.

The ‘N’ word was such a common epithet during the American Civil war that even members of the military elite felt the scourge of the offensive term. General John J Pershing who served with the black “Buffalo Soldiers” of the 10th Cavalry regiment was nicknamed “Nigger Jack” and looked down upon by white cadets because he was known to have referred to this black cohort as 'real soldiers'. Even when he later moved to West Point to work as an instructor, the nickname "Nigger Jack" followed him.

The Negro Cavalry made up of six all African – American army units, were formed on September 21st 1866 at Fort Levenworth, Kansas and were given the name Buffalo soldiers by Native Indian tribes against whom they fought on the frontier. The Apache Indians first coined this term, because they thought these dark skinned men with kinky, curly hair reminded them somewhat of the herds of bison. In turn, the white soldiers are known to have somewhat excoriatingly referred to their Native American foes as "Red Niggers!".

In 1939, even the acclaimed crime author Agatha Christie found a place in her enormously successful literary work for the 'N' word when she published the book entitled "Ten Little Niggers" with complete impunity in Britain utterly oblivious to, or uncaring of any offence it might cause.

In the USA however, they shied away from this title, employed a degree of temperance, and instead called it "And Then There Were None". Today, nothing or very little is ever said about the original naming of the book and I have no doubt that there are many people that remain unaware of the fact. Also often entitled as "Ten Little Indians", the original title was taken from an American minstrel song made famous by a group of white performers in Black Face which bore reference to slaves being described as "Happy little Darkies" and gave a false impression that subjugated blacks were actually happy to be enslaved.

Research suggests that racism in all parts of Europe has its roots in slavery and colonialism. UK history documents that from as early as the 15th Century, and right up to the date of its abolition in 1834, much of Britain's own trading of African slaves was conducted from the coastal areas of Plymouth, Topsham, Exeter, Bristol and Falmouth in Cornwall. One wonders whether these facts in any way explain the often described "regional bias" in those localities as a form of historically learned behaviour.

In spite of these retrospective examples, as we all move forward in enlightened times, the "N" word is very much alive and kicking and is readily employed, particularly in places where there are no ears to hear or eyes to see, or with unashamed abandon.

During one of my many visits to New York during the 80's I was staying with one of my sons when to my astonishment I noted that many of his friends greeted each other enthusiastically with terms like: "What's up nigger?" or "How you doing nigger?" I later learned that black males in "the hood" as they call it, tend to regard this use of the N word as their way of "reclaiming" the revolting epithet as their own. In conversation with a couple of them one evening I suggested that it might not be such a good idea to want to take ownership of such terminology given its early origins and meaning. Needless to say, they both looked at me as if I were crazy and I'm pretty damn sure I heard one of them mutter the word "fool" as they swaggered away, gangster limping as they went with the waistband of their pants halfway down their thighs.

Established film directors like Quentin Tarantino and Spike Lee are well known for spraying the N word around like bullets in movies such as Jackie Brown, Mo' Better Blues and Do the Right Thing. It's a much discussed fact that Samuel L Jackson used the term "nigger" no less than thirty eight times in Jackie Brown, which for me, did nothing but ruin an otherwise entertaining and compelling movie. In Django Unchained, which is set against the backdrop of slave trading in the antebellum period before the American Civil War, the characters used the word so liberally that it prompted one of his fellow film makers to conclude that Tarantino is "simply infatuated" with the word.

What I found particularly distasteful about the film, was the scene where Leonardo Di Caprio, produced the skull of one of his former slaves, and smashing it with a hammer, pointed to three indentations at the base which he claimed every negro bore, and which were said to be responsible for submissiveness.

One can understand how myths such as this could become food and drink for the average redneck watching the film and giggling with glee and spluttering into their popcorn.

As a race of people who have ended up in foreign countries, whether it is Britain, America or Canada, many of us have grown weary and tired of being asked to "play the white man", a patronising term I came across during my formative years which in essence meant, just play the game, don't make any waves. I once asked an avid football fan why he made monkey chants and racially abused black players on the opposing team, even throwing bananas at them, but enthusiastically cheered on the black players in his own team. I was flabbergasted to hear his reply. **"Well, our own black players are Honorary White Men aren't they?"** He offered me this gem of information with a huge grin and a look of manic self-importance. I have to confess that I am not easily surprised by anything, but the fact that he could deliver this bizarre explanation with that amount of hubris and cluelessness left me absolutely dumbfounded.

All this proves is that racism isn't as much a football problem as much as it is a social, societal and generational one. Young lads on the terraces witness their fathers and other groups of spectators mete out this type of racist vitriol week in and week out and see it as "normal" behaviour. It's sad to say but the saying "The apple never falls far from the tree" has never been more appropriate. Despite the efforts of the many sporting bodies worldwide introducing schemes such as Kick it Out and Say No To Racism, the issue is proving to be an extremely hard nut to crack. Trying to drive racism off the terraces or indeed off the internet, is proving to be as impossible a task as nailing jelly to a brick wall.

Once again, like bullies, these so called "fans" on the terraces, are often a group of beer swilling, like-minded louts that constitutes a mere fraction of the thousands attending a match, and who, if confronted one on one would most likely be as meek as a church mouse and probably with the brains to match.

Believe it or not, the barracking and baiting of black players was prevalent and widespread even during the earliest parts of the 20th Century.

Walter John Daniel Tull was born in 1888 and became only the third player of mixed race heritage behind goalkeeper Arthur Wharton and Billy Coles of Aston Villa to represent England. He played for Clapton, Tottenham and Northampton between the years of 1909 and 1917. It was, however when he played for Bristol City that he suffered such a level of abuse from spectators that he was often substituted or even left on the bench for the entire game. The local Football Star newspaper once described the tirade of foul language aimed at him as "lower than Billingsgate", referencing a well known fish market.

Tull was born in Folkstone, Kent, the son of Daniel, a Barbadian born carpenter and descendant of a slave, and an English mother, Alice Elizabeth Palmer. He later joined the British Army and was commissioned as a lieutenant in May 1917, the first black officer ever to be placed in charge of white soldiers during the Great War of 1914 -18. He died during the First Battle of Bapaume, France on March 25th 1918.

His body was never recovered, but his service to his country on the fields of sport and of military conflict has never been forgotten and has since been rightly commemorated in several ways including having commemorative coins struck in his honour.

On Thursday 14th November 2019, the England football team played their One Thousandth international match and, apart from the 7 nil drubbing of the opposing team, it was encouraging to see that the Football Association made a point of marking the occasion by publicly acknowledging the so called "93", that first cohort of black footballers such as, Tull, Arthur Wharton, Viv Anderson, Luther Blissett, Paul Parker, John Barnes to name but a few, who were honoured to pull on the England shirt and in so doing blazed a trail for many others to follow.

Another example of bizarre racially charged vitriol was a heated argument I witnessed between two men, one white the other black which ended with the former ending the dispute with the words: **"F- -k Off, you black c – nt!".** He then called out a female's name and, his girlfriend, *a black girl,* emerged from the crowd, took his hand and off they went together, laughing and joking.

I can vividly recall many occasions when dating an English girl, one would get the impression that they were looking upon you as something of a curiosity. Look, but don't touch. Touch, but don't taste. Enjoy, but don't tell anyone. Treated like an exotic creature, to be sampled but yet kept hidden well out of sight, a kind of novelty or guilty pleasure, somewhat akin to that bit of chocolate (pardon the pun) or fancy cake that one craves for when one *really* should no better ; something for the purpose of entertainment but not to be taken too seriously. One date was only too happy to invite me into her home on more than one occasion "for a coffee", but only on the condition that I agreed to go out onto the landing of the fire escape, or into another room if her father showed up unexpectedly and wait until he had gone. She went on to add that he didn't even like her going out with anyone Greek or Turkish so he would probably burst a blood vessel if he saw me sitting there with my feet tucked cosily under his daughter's table.

This situation is in no way unique. I've known a Bajan girl who secretly dated a Turkish boy for several years unbeknown to the parents of the young man. Similarly, Luisa, a young Italian girl stubbornly dated a black Cuban guy for years despite protestations from her family. In both cases, whilst these couples were clearly extremely fond of each other, they all knew that at some point the relationships would have to end in order for Italian or Turkish family "honour" or cultural protocols to be satisfied. It is no exaggeration to say that a deep faith-based, traditional Muslim family whose son or daughter either had the temerity or naivety to bring home a "Ghorrie", or a "Calloo" (white or black person) and present them as a potential spouse, would be, let's say, less than pleased and would be extremely unlikely to run up and down the front garden doing several cartwheels of joy. More likely, that apocalyptic event would reverberate through the entire community and no doubt have far-reaching consequences.

In the case of my own experiences more often than not, it felt rather like being an item in a store with someone trying on that item knowing full well that they had absolutely no intention of buying it. In essence, one became a phallus with a person somewhat inconveniently attached or a "hail and ride, hop on, hop off" service. No commitment or longevity was sought nor offered, only entertainment of the fleshy kind, whenever it was required or convenient.

Females like these were desperate not to let their friends or family know they had "taken a walk on the dark side". When going on a date, one would ask: ***"Would you mind if we go out somewhere in Hatfield perhaps or up the West End – just in case we bump into someone who knows me?"***

Another girl, in conversation, remarked that I would be *"really good looking if* I *was white"* quote. Now I am sure that in her naivety she may even have meant this as a kind of inappropriately thought out compliment, and I have to admit that at the time I took it as such and didn't give it much thought until many days later. In all of these cases, I put these comments and behaviours down to the individual's upbringing, which are in many ways the same type of parental conditioning which my little buddy Thomas displayed when we were eight years old.

And so the world turns, and we are now living in what is often described as a "mix and match" society, one which is inevitably going to become even more mixed and diverse with relaxed borders and the increased movement of people from all parts of the world. Even the advertising companies appear to have had a reality check judging by the number of adverts on television featuring black and interracial couples of all permutations, thereby dragging that racial hot potato kicking and screaming into the 21st Century.

There will, however, always be those who are steadfast in their reluctance to accept the difference in others instead of championing and welcoming diversity. The sad reality is that if you are black, yellow, fat, skinny, ginger headed or of another religion, someone at some stage will find a reason or opportunity to attach a name or comment to that difference.

As controversial as it may sound the truth is this: It seems that there is only one way that people of differing colours, races and ethnicities are ever going to escape the foul attention of racists and bigots, together with the discrimination and abuse that goes with it, and that is to, wherever possible, stay in one's own country of origin. Unless there are unavoidable reasons for one to migrate, such as fleeing from persecution in one's own land, your country has been decimated by war, or you have suffered irreparable family break down and you are desperate for a fresh start elsewhere, it has to be the correct choice to stay put amongst your own people in the land of your origin.

It is a sad and worrying indictment that in this, the 21st Century, racial divisions around the world are widening again partly due to a particular incumbent of the White House who instead of using his position to bring people together, chose to embrace white nationalism, misogyny and anti-Islamic rhetoric to titillate his narrow base of support. Equally concerning are the seemingly never ending conflicts between Arabs and Jews in the Middle East alongside the backdrop of violence between factions of the same religion. It appears impossible for Sufi, Wahabi, Shia and Sunni Muslims to find common ground, let alone live in peace with those of other faiths and cultures. Proxy wars continue as Kurds and Turks continue to vie for territorial superiority in Syria and Iraq and the persecution of Christians around the world and minority sects such as the Uighurs in China is on the increase. The world is truly in a state of flux and has probably never been a more dangerous place to live in.

In the UK, the Brexit related matters of Britain's attempt at leaving the European Union has caused such divisions that has left some people totally confused about what it means. The campaign which was fought largely on an anti-immigration, take back control platform, has even seen bigots crawl out their hiding places and utter inappropriate comments such as: ***"We're leaving the European Union, so you can all f- -K off back to your own countries now!",*** to black people who have been residing legally in England for more than 50 years.

It's immediately apparent that due to a combination of political naivety, misinformation and having only one brain cell, that this person is either unaware that the Caribbean isn't actually a part of Europe or simply doesn't give a damn and simply wishes to be an offensive dick.

There have been numerous occasions when someone chose to refer to me, not by name, but instead by a word which reflected the hue of my skin. It is true to say that whilst I sometimes rose to the bait, that I eventually found, and still find to this day, that the best way to deal with these challenges is to try and "*go high, whenever someone goes low*", as a politician recently remarked during a particularly rancorous campaign. Wise words indeed.

As a race, we have now learned that it is better to proudly celebrate our difference and brush off any attack of any type, as one would flick dirt or dust from one's shoulder.

CHAPTER TWENTY FOUR

All Lives Matter, Don't They?

Ever since the acquittal of Trayvon Martin's killer in 2013 followed by the slaying of Michael Brown by a white police officer in Ferguson, Missouri 2014, the phrase "black lives matter" has become a loud cry in a new chapter for black freedom and civil rights. The list of names is too long to mention all of them, but those of Eric Garner, Breonna Taylor, George Floyd in the USA and Sean Rigg and Mark Duggan in the UK are burned into our memories due to the protests which followed their deaths at the hands of police.

The Black Lives Matter movements in the USA and its British arm, have on occasion both regrettably been often known for disruptive protests instead of holding accountable those responsible for acts of inequality and challenging incidents of social injustice against members of black communities.

The Movement has often been accused of only reacting fervently when, for example, a black member of the public has reportedly been killed by someone white. This has been further compounded in those few cases where the perpetrators have later been proven to have been black, upon which the protesters have always disappeared from the streets as quickly as they appeared. Don't these lives matter?

In one incident a young black youth was chased by police in Hackney, the very borough in which I grew up. He was apprehended and restrained but unfortunately died later in the hospital of asphyxiation having swallowed a small package he had put in his mouth during the altercation. Clearly questions needed to be asked and answers given, but again following several impassioned public speeches and marches by the BLM movement, an irresponsible and opportune group of youths seized the opportunity to take over the high streets of Dalston and confront the police in the most violent manner possible, hurling bricks, bottles and causing untold damage to shops, and other businesses. They were completely oblivious to the fact that those police in the thin blue line trying to keep order, black and white alike, were merely doing their jobs in trying to keep the peace.

There is an obvious disconnect between a proportion of the police force and their attitude to black males here in the UK and in America. This is borne out by the number of black men who die as a result of either being restrained or shot. As a result, the lack of trust in the police is not only totally diminished already but made even worse by videos which are there for all to see on the internet such as the one where an American police officer is heard telling a nervous white motorist pulled over with the reassuring words: **"Don't worry, we only shoot black people!"** Tongue in cheek comment, or a regrettable sign of the times?

Another frequently asked question is: why do the BLM groups not protest violently in the case of black on black killings in their own communities, after all, figures show that ninety per cent of black murder victims are killed by other black people. Do these black lives matter more than white lives lost in a similar fashion? Data also evidence that eighty four percent of white murder victims are killed by other white people proving that most violent crime is in fact intra-racial.

When injustices occur, black members of communities, precisely the same as their white counterparts, have an inherent right to be outraged, ask questions, hold the perpetrators to account and to seek justice. However, their actions in all cases need to be orderly, measured, proportionate and above all, need to be conducted in ways that do not allow groups of thugs with hidden or personal agendas the opportunity to trash and destroy the very fabric of many neglected, under-resourced and struggling boroughs like Hackney and Haringey. Movements like BLM are right in drawing attention to incidents of wrongdoing and seeking accountability but they need to be wary of those who may attach themselves in order to use such occasions for purely negative reasons.

It can be done, as evidenced by the reaction of a local community in America more recently following the shooting of a young black male who was confronted by two men while out jogging. The response was understandably angry and vociferous but also controlled, and allowed the investigative and lawful processes to move forward in the right way.

Another huge area of concern is the spiralling and disproportionate number of black youths from our inner cities who are losing their lives as a result of either being shot or stabbed. This senseless waste of life is widely believed to emanate from gang culture and connected loyalties. They are also a sad indictment of broken communities, poor living conditions, low aspiration, and indicative of the victims and perpetrators having truly lost their way. These lives matter too.

Week after week we hear people vacillating about the need for more police on the ground and more youth clubs. The blame for the level of lawlessness is placed firmly on government cuts to policing and youth services when in truth it just isn't that simple. It is true that an increase in both, together with hypothetically putting the additional resource of a policeman outside every inner city chicken shop and school might just broker a modicum of success, but the truth is that the young people who wish to avail themselves of after school clubs, mentoring groups, sports, music and educational facilities know exactly where to access them.

The grooming and coercion of very young children into gang-related crime, and others barely into their teens, takes place in many settings, often in or around youth facilities. Once in a gang, it is often nigh on impossible for a disillusioned member to get out without putting themselves at great risk. What is needed therefore is a more holistic approach such as one recently suggested of creating so called "safe houses" where youngsters wishing to escape from gang culture can be placed, protected and supported in a safe environment in which they can be provided with education, training and the tools to change and improve their lives.

Even though gangs don't always consist of strictly racial groups and can often be multi-racial, it seems that the biggest threat to a young black male is indeed another young black male.

To demonstrate the attitude of these youths who have chosen, or been coerced into this way of life, of dealing in and running drugs across so called "County Lines", just consider the words of one such young man I spoke with recently when it became evident that he was using several different mobile phones, I asked him what line of work he was in, he replied: ***"I may not have a job officially, but my work keeps me very busy – the hustle never stops bro'!"***

Clearly such lifestyle choices come with risks, but as we all know, everyone has free will to choose a particular path for themselves even though those choices may well be to the detriment of the individual or others.

CHAPTER TWENTY FIVE

WHERE ALL SONGS END.

"Tomorrow is promised to no one,
Make good use of Today,
Like a flower snapped in the breeze, he swayed
And floundered against the elements,
'til the swirling winds of time
called him home"

Dad died back in 1983. After years of self-neglect brought on by paranoid schizophrenia, he fell in his bathroom and lay stuck between the toilet bowl and the bathtub for two days before I found him there, after I decided to pay him a totally unplanned visit. The fall didn't kill him. He died of pneumonia after spending three months in St Anne's Hospital.

The social workers and doctors had already decided that he clearly wasn't coping at home and were actively considering residential care for him. He had always refused to allow carers in when they arrived to assist him to wash, dress and prepare meals. A couple of years before, the local council even had to resort to having him sectioned and removed to a psychiatric hospital for two weeks in order for them to gain access to his property in order to renovate it. Now, here he was again in a hospital, and I think he knew he wasn't going to be allowed back home this time. Weeks before he passed away, he would tell me that he had "seen" friends from his childhood standing at the foot of his bed.

I recall going to view dad's body at the funeral home and I have to admit that it was an unnerving experience. Upon entering thc chapel, the first thing I noticed was the coffin lying in the middle of the room. The lid had been placed upright against the wall facing the door and bore a brass plate with dad's date of birth and date of death inscribed on it.

I walked slowly up the coffin and upon placing both of my hands on the rim, I peered in and looked down at the body of my father, dressed in the clothes which I had provided the funeral home with. It was a strange experience looking at what seemed to be a strange facsimile of Dad. I don't think anything prepares anyone for looking upon the form of a dead relative. Although I knew it was him, my mind tried to reject the fact and struggled to comprehend that here was this former, enigmatic, insecure and often cruel man lying alone, cold and with nowhere to go other than into the damp, dark earth.

Somewhat tentatively, I reached forward and gently touched his right hand which was placed over his left. It was cold, so cold.

His funeral was a quiet affair, followed by a cremation service. For a reading, I had chosen a well known poem entitled "Remember me", by Christine Rosetti, the words of which, with their sensitivity and honesty, provided me with a degree of solace then and in years to come. After collecting his ashes, I kept them for many weeks on a shelf in my bedroom, probably for around two months and would have kept them for much longer had my mum not remarked: **"You can't keep him up there forever you know!"**

She was right of course, so we had them interred in a small plot at the local Crematorium in Brunswick Park.

Mum's condition worsened over the ensuing years until after many crises caused by all of the daily problems associated with severe dementia, cognitive impairment, weight loss through not eating, together with the inability to manage her finances to name a few, she was referred to a psycho-geriatrician who recommended immediate admission to a nursing home in Christchurch.

During mum's final two years, during that dark period of mental incapacity and vulnerability, I regret to say that she was shamelessly abused and neglected by many people she would have been relying on for support and protection. The most heinous form of abuse was the embezzlement of thousands of pounds from an account we opened for her due to her habit of losing her debit cards or simply failing to remember the pin number. The thieves, more akin to a pack of ravenous jackals than human beings, had a field day. After discovering the code to the cash machine they used her card to make several withdrawals a day from the account containing sixty two thousand dollars over a 6 month period until only 44 dollars remained in the account. I must note that much to their eternal shame, the staff of her bank in St James were completely unhelpful, even when the fraudulent abuse was brought to their attention. How a modern day bank could fail to notice the frequent number of daily withdrawals only serves to highlight their total incompetence and negligence. Apart from somewhat grudgingly providing me with statements, they did nothing. Furthermore, We even had to take a rather costly flight over to Barbados to get the statements in person as the manager refused to email scanned copies to us.

Being overseas when the abuse took place, which was extremely convenient for the perpetrators, it remained difficult to lay absolute blame on any one person or group, but the saying "the eyes are the windows to the soul" tells it like it is. When I looked into the eyes of the many who were close to her, one knew immediately where answers lie and it goes without saying that a price will be paid, in this lifetime or the next.

Upon being placed in nursing care she actually rallied for a while, even putting on some weight after receiving much long overdue care and treatment. One of the reasons for her short-lived improvement apart from the excellent care and environment, was the advanced delusional state she was in, which led her to believe that she was actually in charge of the home and the staff, which filled her waking hours with a great deal of satisfaction. Whenever we visited her, her eyes would light up with joy whenever she imparted snippets of information about particular members of the care staff. She would point them out and tell us in detail how she had "trained" them and how she "supervises" their work.

Sad to say that after only eight months in The Retreat, as it is called, she contracted a chest infection and after spending a week in Queen Elizabeth Hospital, she eventually succumbed to a pulmonary embolism and passed away aged 84.

Her funeral and burial at Coral Ridge Memorial Gardens, Christchurch, was a grand affair with mum's casket taking pride of place at the entrance to the chapel where the service was held. It seemed that even in death, mum was not to be ignored. Resplendent in her favourite colour green, she looked serene and at peace. And of course, we made sure the ashes of her beloved Minnie were there with her in the casket.

The Reverend Tyrone who performed the eulogy, spoke passionately about mum having been a feisty and combative woman who had been resolute in not standing for any nonsense in either her personal nor her professional life.

He informed the congregation how my mum and dad, like many others, came to England during the period of the 1950's that came to be known as the "Windrush Years". A bleak time in history for immigrants looking for a new life in the Mother Country, England. A time when, upon seeking accommodation, black people were greeted by signs in windows stating :

"NO BLACKS, NO IRISH, NO DOGS!"

The service itself was a long affair, with many readings and hymns, culminating with the procession behind the casket out of the chapel out to the graveside where there were even more readings. Mum's funeral was never going to be a short one. Eventually, the time came for the interment and the moment I had so dreaded. There is something terribly final about watching a loved one's casket disappear out of view and into the ground. This was made excruciatingly more painful by the sound of the casket eventually coming to rest on the hard, rocky floor of the grave.

It is then that you truly understand that you will never see that person again.

The philosophical truth about death is that it is an inescapable part of that cycle of existence followed by non- existence. No one escapes it. The slab in a mortuary and then the cemetery is where most, if not all of us, will end up.

All we can aim for in life is that we do as much good and as little wrong as possible and that we have a good, peaceful, pain-free end.

Poem: Where All Songs End

When I am laid deep and far down in the earth, and my body no longer bears value or worth.

Have kind thoughts of me often, or whenever you can, for life slips from us all like grains of fine sand.

Man born of woman, is imperfect and weak, and life doesn't give us all that we seek.

And though here I lie, unmoving and cold, remember how I once walked, confident and bold.

Grieve not for this soul, in the end all must part, keep fond memories of me, close in your heart.

There is a place for the living, and a place for the dead, as frequently written, and so often said.

No need for sadness, no need to weep, I am merely resting in eternal sleep.

Though the flesh is no more, something remains, that breeze through your hair, that one drop of rain.

That small piece of soil which sticks to your shoe, a little bit of me is always with you.

CHAPTER TWENTY SIX

The Final Analysis

Those of us who are the children or grandchildren of the Windrush generation, an invited but somewhat displaced group of people, owe our forbears an undeniably huge debt of gratitude for all they endured. The harsh insults, the pain of rejection, the open hostility and discrimination, the denial of hope and opportunities.

We owe them so much, for taking it all on their shoulders and for somehow finding a way through it all, to carve an easier route through which we could navigate, and in so doing, provided us with the chance of having a far better experience.

And so, this message goes out to a section of today's young black males: Your forefathers and mothers paid a huge price and made several sacrifices in order to leave you a hard-earned legacy of tremendous opportunities.

Be aware that you *will* continue to be pre-judged in many instances. Because of the skin colour you are in, it is the first thing a bigoted and ignorant person with preconceived beliefs sees.

A prominent black politician once wrote that black youths should "pull their pants up". He was, of course, referring to the somewhat unfortunate style adopted by many young black males, of "sagging", or wearing one's pants so low that the undergarments are on show. People will judge you on this shabby display because that is what it is, shabby. It isn't cool, trendy or masculine to wear your pants below your buttocks thereby displaying your grubby underwear. This style of dress originated in the American prison service purely by circumstance and should never have been embraced so readily as a fashion statement. Even some white youths have followed this pattern of swaggering along with buttocks on show and with a hand down the front of their pants groping their genitals, "hand muff" style as it is sometimes called, in an effort to "look cool". Be careful not to shake those hands as they come with a health warning. The advice to this legion of wayward youth is this: Pull up your pants, take pride in your appearance, have belief in your abilities and aim as high as you can. Throw away the knife and the gun and engage proactively with your communities by making positive contributions.

The challenges presented by the hue of your skin doesn't mean that you have to be contained or restricted by your colour or racial origin. Many youths who complain of an absence of positive role models in their lives through circumstance, or those who seek inspiration, are often encouraged to look only as far as figures such as Rosa Parks, Mary Seacole, Martin Luther King, Darcus Howe, Nelson Mandela, Barack Obama, Tiger Woods, Arthur Ashe, The Williams Sisters, The Black Farmer, Lewis Hamilton and Muhammad Ali to name but a few.

It is true that all of the aforementioned stood up for, against, or achieved something of tremendous magnitude in the face of fierce opposition, or in fields they were not expected to excel in. However, some of those achievements, as laudable as they may be, need to be tempered by some caveats. For example, while Obama was and still is looked upon as a charming and affable man with enviable oratorial skills, he will also be regarded by many as having been a rather ineffectual president during his two terms in office, largely due to obstructionist, partisan politics by the opposing Republican Party. What cannot be denied, however, is that he, against huge odds managed to become the first, and possibly the only, black commander in chief of the most powerful nation in the free world, and went on to achieve two terms in office despite the Republicans trying every way possible to make him a 'one term' president.

Similarly, the successes in elite sports such as golf, motor racing and tennis by the many notable black sportsmen and women are all the more remarkable and rare because of the huge amount of cash needed with which, not only to get started in, but with which to maintain competitiveness. Sadly, there is often a huge degree of travel between hopeful aspiration and actual achievement.

In today's media driven world where so many people conduct their lives through a camera lens constantly searching for the perfect selfie, the average youngster from a poor inner city background is, therefore, unlikely to gain a foothold in these hallowed sporting areas, so while they will always have such heroes to look up to, their inspiration needs to come from deep within themselves. They should, therefore, aim for what is truly practical and achievable and above all, always have a back-up plan for something less spectacular, just in case that pot of gold at the end of a rainbow doesn't materialise. There is no shame in that. Making a contribution to the country, community and family is what counts.

It is said that "many are called but few are chosen", but this doesn't mean that because one can't do *everything* that one shouldn't try *something.*

Don't allow your spirit to be crushed: view each challenge as a character building exercise with which to brush aside the many obstacles which may be strewn across the paths before you.

Although they may be many, persevere, and with providence, opportunity, and also a little luck at times, one will have a much better chance of reaching those elusive goals.

Don't waste precious mental energy in hating those who endeavour to put obstacles in your way. Hatred is an emotion which festers and grows, is all consuming and which, if left unchecked, can eventually destroy that which contains it.

A vessel doesn't sink because of the water it is in, but because of the water that gets into it.

With the planting and nurturing of a few more seeds of hope and tolerance, we may well discover that as individuals, there is far more that binds us than that which divides us.

One will never be able to change what was, so it is far better for us to accept what is, and have belief, faith and hope for what can be. And if anyone can bring about change – If not us, then who.

And if not now – when?

Lightning Source UK Ltd.
Milton Keynes UK
UKHW021523100820
367992UK00012B/2950